THE ROUGH GUIDE TO

Tutankhamun

THE KING : THE TREASURE : THE DYNASTY

ROUGH GUIDE CREDITS

Text Editor: Mark Ellingham
Design/layout: Link Hall
Picture research: Suzanne Bosman
Cover design: Diana Jarvis
Proofreader: Daniel Crewe
Production: Aimee Hampson

PUBLISHING INFORMATION

This first edition published June 2005, revised June 2007
by Rough Guides Ltd,
80 Strand, London WC2R oRL

Distributed by the Penguin Group:
Penguin Books Ltd, 80 Strand, London WC2R oRL.
Penguin Putnam, Inc. 375 Hudson Street, New York 10014, USA
Penguin Group (Australia), 250 Camberwell Road, Camberwell, Victoria 3124, Australia
Penguin Books Canada Ltd, 10 Alcorn Avenue,
Toronto, Ontario, Canada M4V 1E4
Penguin Group (New Zealand), Cnr Rosedale and Airborne Roads, Albany, Auckland, New
Zealand

Typeset in Bernhard Modern, Metaplus and Garamond.
Printed in Italy by Legoprint S.p.A.

224pp includes index
A catalogue record for this book is available from the British Library.

1 3 5 7 9 8 6 4 2

ISBN 9-781-84353-865-3

THE ROUGH GUIDE TO

Tutankhamun

Written and researched by
Michael Haag

To Colin and Julia Elgie,

in appreciation of our friendship

CONTENTS

Tutankhamun

THE KING : THE TREASURE : THE DYNASTY

When Howard Carter discovered the tomb of Tutankhamun in 1922, he opened a door onto the golden age of the pharaohs, that era of grandeur, opulence and empire known as the New Kingdom, which began with the kings of the 18th Dynasty. Overlooked by graverobbers for more than 3000 years, the long-lost tomb in the Valley of the Kings yielded a treasure of unimagined magnificence. 'Wonderful things', Carter exclaimed as his eyes adjusted to the light from his flickering candle, 'strange animals, statues and gold – everywhere the glint of gold'.

But the appeal of Tutankhamun is not just about treasures. He was born into one of the most dramatic moments of Egyptian history, a time of religious, political and artistic revolution which reached its peak during the reign of Akhenaten, who with his strikingly beautiful wife Nefertiti purged Egypt of its old gods and introduced the world's first monotheistic religion. After the death of Akhenaten, who was probably Tutankhamun's father, the boy king found himself in the hands of contending forces, among them the powerful priesthood of Amun, the king of the gods, who wanted to return to the old polytheistic religion. The intrigue and mystery surrounding Tutankhamun's throne, and his unexpectedly premature death, contribute to the fascination and drama of this period.

This *Rough Guide to Tutankhamun* is a comprehensive introduction to the king, the treasure and the dynasty. It begins by describing the significance of objects in The Exhibition, most of which have come from 18th Dynasty tombs in the Valley of the

Kings, and especially from the tomb of Tutankhamun, the only New Kingdom royal tomb ever found intact. **The Search for Tutankhamun** follows: the story of how the tomb was discovered by Howard Carter, backed by his patron Lord Carnarvon, reads like a 1920s detective story and concludes with a discussion of the famous curse. The guide then provides the historical framework for Tutankhamun: an account of the **18th Dynasty** pharaohs and their capital of Thebes, home to the kings and to the powerful priesthood of Amun, which during the reign of Amenophis III was the greatest city in the ancient world. At the height of its glory, Akhenaten, the heretic pharaoh, abandoned the city, closed its temples, and established the worship of his one god, the Aten – a presage, say some, of Judeo-Christian monotheism. It is this that makes the period of Tutankhamun so compelling, with his role in Egypt's 'counter reformation', restoring Amun and the old priesthoods, followed by sudden death and hasty burial in a makeshift tomb. Was he murdered? The most modern evidence is discussed, including the results of the CT scan of Tutankhamun's mummy undertaken in 2005.

Background chapters follow on **Tombs and afterlife**, looking at the religious beliefs inherent in tomb burial, the activities of tomb robbers, and the process of mummification. And a final **Resources** section includes reviews of books and websites, and a glossary for Ancient Egyptian terms.

1. The Exhibition

Tutankhamun and the Golden Age of the Pharaohs

Tutankhamun's diadem is one of the exhibition highlights. It is shown here as discovered in its original tomb location.

Tutankhamun and the Golden Age of the Pharaohs

AN INTRODUCTION TO THE EXHIBITION

The term 'blockbuster exhibition' was born when the **Treasures of Tutankhamun** visited Britain and America and Britain in the 1970s. That exhibition included Tutankhamun's solid gold funeral mask, several gold or gilded statues of the king, gods and sacred animals, as well as vases, lamps, jewellery, furniture and other objects for the afterlife. The magnificent funeral trappings of the boy-king, combined with the age-old fascination with ancient Egypt, generated an immense response. When the fifty artefacts from Tutankhamun's tomb were put on show at London's British Museum, over 1.6 million people came to see them in six months, many of them queuing for eight hours round the block. There were similar scenes during the exhibition's three-year American tour. Nearly a million people came to see the treasures in the four months they were on display at the National Gallery of Art in Washington DC, and when the exhibition travelled on to Chicago, New Orleans, Los Angeles, Seattle, San Francisco and New York, the legendary finds drew seven million more.

Now 'Tut is back', in the words of Zahi Hawass, Secretary General of Egypt's Supreme Council of Antiquities. This new exhibition, **Tutankhamun and the Golden Age of the Pharaohs**, has made a 27-month tour of America, starting in Los Angeles in 2005 and continuing on to Fort Lauderdale, Chicago and Philadelphia, before crossing the Atlantic to Britain in 2007.

A New Museum for Egypt

There were those in Egypt who objected to another Tutankhamun tour, fearing damage to the artefacts or their irreplaceable loss. But they changed their minds when told of the greater danger facing Tutankhamun's treasures which, except for a few objects at the Luxor Museum and the remains of Tutankhamun himself in a gilded coffin in his tomb in the Valley of the Kings, are normally on display at the **Egyptian Museum in Cairo**. A venerable century-old institution, the museum was built in peaceful grounds near the banks of the Nile in 1902. Cairo has grown tremendously since then, however, and the museum now finds itself in the midst of the city, where it suffers from traffic vibration and pollution. It desperately needs modernisation, and the collection also needs more room.

The Egyptian authorities have therefore decided to build a new state-of-the-art **Grand Egyptian Museum** out by the Great Pyramids of Giza on the edge of the Western Desert, well away from the centre of Cairo. The old museum will be refurbished and will display monumental stone statues and other large objects of the Old and New Kingdoms. But most of its contents will be transferred to the new museum, including the entire treasures of Tutankhamun, which will be given pride of place – though not before he sings for his supper, as a chief purpose of the present tour is to raise money to help meet the cost of constructing the new Grand Egyptian Museum.

The atrium of the Egyptian Museum in Cairo in 1903, as exhibits were being installed. Pride of place went to the colossal statue of Amenophis III and Queen Tiy, the parents of Akhenaten and probable grandparents of Tutankhamun.

At the embalming of Tutankhamun, his organs were removed, mummified. and given small coffinettes of their own. This is one – and it displays his features.

THE GOLDEN AGE OF THE PHARAOHS EXHIBITION

The Tutankhamun and the Golden Age of the Pharaohs exhibition is not simply a repetition of the 1970s tour. Again there are fifty artefacts from the tomb of Tutankhamun, but many of these are different to those seen before. They include the king's **royal diadem**, the gold crown discovered encircling the head of Tutankhamun's mummified body, and one of the gold and inlaid **Canopic coffinettes** that contained his mummified internal organs. Furthermore, they are joined by an additional eighty objects from other tombs in the Valley of the Kings and from elsewhere. Altogether, they are among the finest artefacts of **18th Dynasty Egypt**.

In this Golden Age exhibition, **Tutankhamun** is the starting point for a wider investigation of the 18th Dynasty burial practices and religious beliefs; the display reaches out to include artefacts from the royal tombs of **Amenophis II**, **Tuthmosis IV** and **Amenophis III**, as well as the tomb of **Yuya and Tuyu**, parents of Amenophis III's wife Queen Tiy.

Also there are artefacts relating to the heretical pharaoh **Akhenaten** and his beautiful wife **Nefertiti** who were the driving force behind the **Amarna revolution** which overturned the established forms of religion, art and royal rule. With Akhenaten's death, if not before, Egypt was plunged into crisis – and this was the inheritance of the boy-king Tutankhamun, whose father is thought to have been Akhenaten himself.

Tutankhamun and the Golden Age of the Pharaohs is therefore an exhibition about the king and about his treasures, but it is also about his family, those last great kings and queens of the 18th Dynasty who raised Egypt to unprecedented heights of splendour before convulsing it in dark confusion until they themselves were buried in the Valley of the Kings.

WHO'S WHO IN THE VALLEY OF THE KINGS

Early on in the 18th Dynasty, when **Thebes** became the capital of Egypt, its kings chose a remote desert valley in the Theban hills for the concealment and protection that it offered to their mummies and their treasures as they began their journey into the afterlife. More than 62 rock-cut tombs have so far been discovered in the **Valley of the Kings**, which contains almost all the tombs of the **New Kingdom pharaohs** – that is those of the **18th, 19th and 20th Dynasties**, from about 1492 BC, when Tuthmosis I was the first to be buried there, to the last, Ramses XI in about 1069 BC. Some others were also granted the privilege of being buried in the Valley, such as the various wives of 18th Dynasty kings, as well as Yuya and Tuyu (who, uniquely in these valley tombs, were commoners – though the parents of Queen Tiy). Children of the kings were not normally buried in the Valley, but there were exceptions, among them the two still-born daughters of Tutankhamun and his wife Ankhesenamun.

Preparing for Eternity

Egyptian religious belief required that the dead were buried with a set of **personal and ritual objects** that they would need in the afterlife. But as the tombs were the receptacles of priceless treasures, they became the target of thieves even in ancient times. In consequence it is extremely rare to find tombs with their grave goods intact, in particular the last resting places of the pharaohs, which were repeatedly broken into over the millennia. It was therefore a sensation when **Howard Carter** discovered the **tomb of Tutankhamun** in 1922. It was the only royal tomb from the New Kingdom to have survived practically entire. The quality shown in the craftsmanship that went into making Tutankhamun's funerary goods of gold and silver and precious stones was astonishing, and they continue to amaze today.

Although almost all the royal tombs were plundered in ancient times, it is possible to reconstruct a list of goods placed within them on the basis of what was found in Tutanhamun's nearly intact tomb, and from the remnants found in the tombs of such other kings as **Amenophis II** and **Tuthmosis IV**, some of whose artefacts are included in the current exhibition. Typically, the **mummified king** was placed within a **coffin** which was enclosed by several more, each nesting within the other like Russian dolls, and these were placed in a stone **sarcophagus** surrounded in turn by a number of gilded wooden **shrines**. A large number of other objects needed for the sustenance, protection and use of the dead king was also placed within the burial chamber. Often the process of stocking the tomb began years before the king's death.

The Mummy

The wrappings wound round the mummy also bound in numerous **pendants, jewels and amulets** which provided protection and magical assistance. The famous **gold mask of Tutanhamun** preserved the image of the king as he was in life, while the various **items and insignia** placed upon him ensured that his rulership would continue in the afterworld.

The Coffin

The mummy was placed in a coffin which in turn was usually placed within several more made of gilded wood or precious metal. 18th Dynasty coffins are anthropoid in shape, that is they are in the form of the human body and symbolically provide an alternative body for the dead king's spirit.

The Sarcophagus

The stone sarcophagus was protected at its corners by the figures of the goddesses **Isis**, **Nephthys**, **Neith** and **Selkis**.

Funerary Shrines

Gilded wooden shrines enclosed the sarcophagus, in the case of Tutankhamun four of them, one within the other. Tutankhamun's shrine was decorated with texts and scenes from the Egyptian **Book of the Dead**.

The Canopic Chest and Containers

Mummification involved the removal of the **internal organs** or viscera – the liver, lungs, stomach and intestines. These were separately embalmed and wrapped and placed in four containers known as **Canopic jars**. Like the sarcophagus, the four protective goddesses stood at the corners of the chest containing the four jars. In the case of Tutankhamun, each set of organs was first placed in a miniature coffin which was then inserted in a jar.

Ritual Figures and Models

Tutankhamun's tomb contained two life-size **ka statues** of himself which guarded the door to the burial chamber. Among the smaller statuettes were **figures of the king** striding, spearing or riding upon the back of a panther. There were also 28 **statues of the gods**, and 413 **shabti figures** representing the field workers necessary for keeping the afterlife ticking over effortlessly. Model hoes and other **agricultural implements** were included so that the shabtis could get on with their work. A **vegetating Osiris** was also a common feature of 18th Dynasty tombs. These were wooden trays in the shape of the god, filled with Nile silt and planted with seeds which were expected to germinate after the tomb had been sealed – to symbolise rebirth and the continuation of life after death. **Model boats and chariots** were also included as a symbolic means of transportation for the king through the underworld, as well as large **ritual couches** on which he could rest.

Objects of Daily Life

Apart from ritual items, many of the objects buried with a king were for practical **daily use in the afterlife** and included clothing, jewellery, cosmetics and perfumes, also games, musical instruments, weaponry, tableware, pottery, furniture of all kinds – including chairs, stools, beds, boxes, chests and baskets – and plentiful supplies of food, such as preserved meats, grain, fruits and copious amounts of beer and wine. And there were family heirlooms and personal mementos, like the **lock of Tiy's hair** found in Tutankhamun's tomb.

Among the items in the exhibition are two **daggers** which Tutankhamun was carrying on his body. One of these is gold, but more significant is the one with an iron blade. It was buried with Tutankhamun because in Egypt at that time **iron** was still a rare and precious metal, though it was becoming more common in the Near East. Egypt finally entered the Iron Age during the 20th Dynasty, that is during the twelfth century BC, but could obtain supplies only in western Asia. But partly because Egypt was short on iron weaponry, its hold on the Near East was slipping. Instead

Egypt had to pay for iron with gold. One reason why tomb robbing became so common during the 20th Dynasty and after was the need to buy iron, and to obtain gold, which the country could no longer afford to leave buried with its dead, to pay for it.

18TH DYNASTY ART

What can seem strange about the Egyptians is their passionate longing for an eternal existence, and yet their expression of it in highly practical and material terms, as though what mattered more than the preparation of their souls was making sure that they had packed their suitcases properly and had not left anything behind. You see something of a reaction against this in the art of the **Amarna period**. Nothing so vividly portrays the break with past conventions than the sculpture and reliefs of **Akhenaten's reign**, which are among the most striking artistic works of ancient Egypt. And yet generally as you go round this exhibition you are time and again charmed by what you see. There is a colourfulness, a gaiety and a playfulness in the art and craftsmanship of the 18th Dynasty that delights the eye and speaks of their own delight in man and nature, and in the joy they found in life – such joy that whether through Amun or Aten they wanted it to last forever.

The Exhibits

A number of items in the exhibition are described below, and their significance is considered. They are arranged in broadly **chronological order**, starting with the tomb of Yuya and Tuyu, through Akhenaten and the Amarna period, and finally to the tomb of Tutankhmun. Note that further items in the exhibition are illustrated and discussed in other chapters of this book.

Tutankhamun's Tomb

This view of Tutankhamun's tomb, below, both shows its structure and indicates the contents of its chambers. The entrance corridor descends to the antechamber. Beyond it is the annexe, while to the right, through a sealed doorway guarded by two life-size figures of the king, is the burial chamber where Tutankhamun lies within his series of coffins, which are set within the sarcophagus, the entire assemblage enclosed by shrines. Off the burial chamber is the treasury in which stood a smaller shrine containing Tutankhamun's Canopic jars.

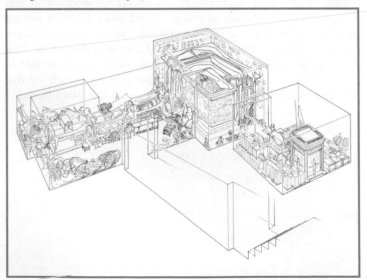

The Coffin of Tuyu

Tuyu was the wife of Yuya, who was commander of the cavalry and its chariot corps under Amenophis III. Chariots were the most up-to-date and powerful weapon in the Egyptian armed forces, which made Yuya a very important man; also he and his wife were the parents of Queen Tiy, the wife of Amenophis III. Both through military service and marriage, Yuya and Tuya were as close to the royal family as commoners could be, which explains why they were favoured with a tomb in the Valley of the Kings.

Five mummiform coffins were found in their tomb, three of them Yuya's, nested one into the other, and two of them Tuyu's, likewise nested. The best preserved of these, and on display at the exhibition, is Tuyu's outer mummiform coffin, which is made of wood, covered with stucco and then gold-plated. The outstretched wings of the goddess Nut, who is depicted beneath Tuyu's magnificently decorated neck, both protect the body and fan it with the breath of life.

A Small Head of Queen Tiy

Tiy was the daughter of Yuya and Tuyu, the wife of Amenophis III and the mother of Akhenaten. This head of a statuette of Queen Tiy made from dark green serpentine was found in a turquoise mining area of Sinai, where Amenophis III had recently enlarged a temple to Hathor. Probably, along with statuettes of Amenophis and other members of their family, this was a votive offering at the temple. The cartouche at the centre of the headpiece confirms her identity, though Tiy is in any case recognisable in her finely worked features, which suggest true portraiture. Her downturned mouth, however, was a stylistic device connoting the weight of responsibility and wisdom. Tiy's shoulder-length wig was the height of fashion during the reign of Amenophis III.

Head from a Colossal Statue of Amenophis IV (Akhenaten)

Before Amenophis IV decamped from Thebes, changed his name to Akhenaten, and built a new capital for the sun god Aten at Akhet-aten (known today as Amarna), he erected one or more vast sanctuaries to Aten just to the east of the temple of Amun at Karnak. Like everything built by Akhenaten, it was destroyed after his death. This head of Amenophis IV, once part of a colossal statue, was found buried at Karnak among other fragments of his work. The four-feathered headdress indicates that the king is associating himself with Shu, god of air and sunlight. His wife Nefertiti joined him in these ceremonies in the role of Tefnut, Shu's sister-twin and wife, and together they formed a triad with their divine father, the androgynous creator god Atum. These statues of Amenophis IV found at Karnak are the first evidence of the radical change in artistic style that is associated with his reign. This Amarna style is not meant to represent the king or others realistically, rather it has religious significance, the sexual ambiguity suggesting that the king possesses the creative powers of both man and woman.

Relief of Akhenaten and his Family with Aten

Akhenaten, wearing an exaggeratedly tall version of the white crown of Upper Egypt, is shown along with Nefertiti making an offering to Aten, which is embodied in the sun disc. Hands at the ends of the sun disc's radiating arms hold the ankh, the sign of life, to the noses of the royal couple. The extreme distortion of the king's figure is typical of the early Amarna style. Not evident in this close-up photograph is the full figure of Nefertiti who makes offering behind the king, and behind her their daughter Meritaten. The heads and body shapes of both women are highly distorted. Nefertiti's transparent dress is open and shows her naked with the intention of stressing her fertility, while Akhenaten's kingly power and virility, all part of his sexually ambivalent appearance, is indicated by the bull's tail hanging down behind him. This relief was part of a balustrade of a ramp rising to an upper storey of the great palace at Akhenaten's capital at Akhet-aten, where it promoted the new idea that the king and his family stood in place of the old deities, whose worship he had banned. Instead, the population was expected to worship Aten through the mediation of the king.

Head of Nefertiti

Though found at Memphis, not at Akhenaten's capital of Akhet-aten, this quartzite head has been identified as definitely a portrait of Nefertiti – but it belongs to the later Amarna period, when high exaggeration gave way to a more subdued and elegant style. The eyes and eyebrows would have been inlaid, possibly with glass, while the broad low tenon at top of the head served to attach a crown or wig, probably of some material other than stone.

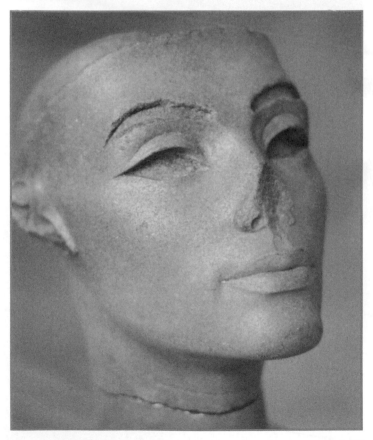

Tutankankhamun's Diadem

The construction of this diadem suggests it was not merely intended for burial with the king, but that it was regularly worn by him in life. As the photo of Tutankhamun's mummy on page 10 indicates, covering the face with the gold mask meant the vulture's head of Upper Egypt and Uraeus cobra of Lower Egypt had first to be removed from the diadem. They were found wrapped to the thighs of the mummy.

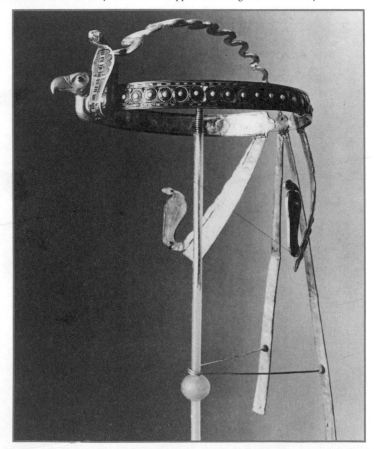

Canopic Jar Lid

Tutankhamun's viscera – his lungs, stomach, intestines and liver — were separately mummified, wrapped and placed in small gold coffinettes which in turn were inserted into Canopic jars made of alabaster, the lid of each supposedly bearing the painted face of the king. One of the coffinettes and one of these portrait lids is shown in the exhibition. But in fact it appears that these Canopic jars, and the chest which contained them, were recycled from someone else's tomb – an expediency which allowed the boy-king's tomb to be rapidly filled with grave goods, despite the unexpectedness of his death and therefore the lack of preparation for his burial. It is estimated that as much as 80 percent of Tutankhamun's core grave goods – those immediately round his body in the burial chamber – were requisitioned from other tombs. Who these jars and their container originally belonged to is uncertain.

Canopic is in fact a misnomer. The word derives from Canopus, a town along the coast from Alexandria which the Greeks named after one of their legendary heroes. It was the seat of a cult of Osiris in which the god was represented as a bulbous jar with a human head, not unlike the jars used by the Egyptians to hold embalmed viscera. Soon the Greeks were not only calling these Osiris jars Canopic jars, but they were confusing them with the jars used to hold internal organs. The confusion was unwittingly picked up by early European antiquarians, and the name has become established usage.

Tutankhamun Mannequin

Howard Carter called this bust of Tutankhamun a mannequin, supposing that it may have served as a dummy for clothes and jewellery. No one has come up with a better explanation, and it is quite possible that it did serve the king's attendants as a device for hanging his ceremonial garb. The bust is made of wood, coated with a layer of stucco, and painted.

Tutankhamun as King of Upper Egypt

Thirty-two gilded wooden statuettes of Tutankhamun were found in his tomb, most of them inside shrines that had been placed in the treasury. The slightly bulging bellies suggest a continuing Amarna influence. In some cases their symbolic purpose is clear: they depict the king in the underworld driving out the forces of chaos in the form of hippopotamuses and snakes – the panther, for example, is the destroyer of snakes. In one case the king is shown wearing the tall white crown of Upper Egypt and carrying those symbols of royal authority, the crook and flail, though in this instance not in their stylised form, rather as a shepherd and a farmer would actually have used them.

[inset] Tutankhamun statuettes, as above, inside the original shrine

Statue of Haroeris

Made of wood and covered with gold leaf, this falcon-headed Haroeris has alert obsidian eyes set into a surround of blue and red inlaid glass. His beak of copper alloy is engraved and painted black, and he wears a full long golden wig which is typical of late 18th Dynasty style. Haroeris was lord of the night sky, and he was expected to ensure the king's ascension into the heavens where he would be transformed into a circumpolar star – one of those stars encircling the North Star, and which never pass below the horizon and therefore never die.

Statue of Ptah

Together with Amun of Thebes and Ra of Heliopolis, Ptah of Memphis was one of the state gods of the New Kingdom. As the god of crafts, he was also associated with the creator god Atum. In addition he had specific funerary functions, as suggested by his feathered costume which gives him a mummified appearance. His task was to ward off the enemies of the dead and to assist in the opening of the mouth ceremony in which the mummy was prepared for accepting offerings of food.

This small statue is intricately worked. The wooden form is covered with reddish gold leaf, though the face is covered with a yellow gold leaf to make it stand out from the rest of the body. The blue cap is of faience, and the eyes are inlaid with white glass and obsidian. He holds a long copper sceptre which carries two symbols at the top: the djed pillar which stands for endurance and stability, and the ankh which stands for life.

Small Statue Shrine

This small shrine was found in the antechamber of Tutankhamun's tomb near the tumble of chariots. It once held a statue of Tutankhamun, but it was looted by ancient tomb robbers. Fortunately they left the shrine behind. Made of wood and covered inside with gold leaf and outside with sheet gold, it is decorated all over with delicate reliefs. The theme is always the same: the king and queen as man and wife. In one scene, illustrated here, Tutankhamun is pouring some sort of liquid into Ankhesenamun's hand. He sits upon a folding stool, an example of which is included in the exhibition, while she rests on a thick padded cushion. The scenes are always intimate and tender and are meant to convey a perfect harmony between them.

Gold Ostrich Feather Fan

An inscription on the handle of the fan says that Tutankhamun himself provided its ostrich feathers when hunting in the desert east of Heliopolis – and indeed the fan-plate is illustrated with that very scene, Tutankhamun racing forward in his chariot, firing arrows at ostriches who are pursued by his Saluki hound. In order to have his hands free, he has tied the reins round his waist. This is precisely how Tutankhamun may have taken a fall, been caught up in the reins, dragged along by his horses and repeatedly pulled under the wheels of his own chariot, causing the fractured leg and missing knee cap discovered in the recent CT scan, which is now suspected of being the cause of his death, through a severe infection.

Ceremonial Shield

Four large shields were found in the annexe of Tutankhamun's tomb. Normally shields were made of wood and covered in hide, and they were carried into battle by both infantry and charioteers alike. But none of these shields was covered in hide, and instead scenes were carved on their open woodwork, which is covered with gold leaf. In this example Tutankhamun is shown in the form of a sphinx trampling over his enemies who from the dress and colour are Nubian princes. Such scenes are conventional, however, and it is unlikely that Tutankhamun had yet been engaged in any military activity.

Crook with Nubian Captive

As with the ceremonial shield, the king used a staff, which symbolises his authority, to illustrate his power in defeating Egypt's enemies and thereby maintaining the divine order. The conquered enemy are always either people of the Near East or Nubians, and again it is a Nubian prince who is shown bound on the handle of this staff.

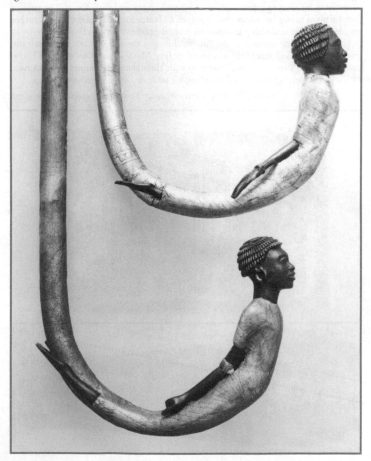

Pectoral with Winged Scarab

This intricately worked pectoral is made of gold, rock crystal, carnelian, feldspar and glass. The scarab represents the sun which in turn symbolises rebirth. The goddesses Nephthys on the left and Isis on the right support the wings of the beetle, whose underside is inscribed with a passage from the Book of the Dead in which the deceased urges his heart to testify in his favour at the weighing of his soul ceremony before Osiris. The pectoral shows signs of having been reworked, however, and careful scrutiny of the inscription had revealed an earlier underlying reference to Aten, the god worshipped by Akhenaten.

Carter found the pectoral in the Anubis shrine in the treasury, but the scarab that goes with it was held separately in a jewellery box. Many items of jewellery and other precious objects were also found bound in with Tutankhamun's mummy, as illustrated by the accompanying photograph showing his body at a stage in its unwrapping.

[below] Mummy of Tutankhamun Showing Amulets, Jewellery, etc.

Mirror Case in the Form of an Ankh

Mirrors were used by Egypt's upper classes, though not of glass, rather of highly polished precious metal. In this case, tomb robbers stole the mirror but left the ankh-shaped case behind, though its wooden form is covered with gold and silver sheet. Mirrors carried religious significance as symbols of regeneration, and of course the ankh is the sign of life. Moreover within the loop of the ankh is a scene depicting a scarab set over an open lotus – again, both are symbols of regeneration.

Silver Trumpet with Wooden Core

Because no system of musical notation was employed by the ancient Egyptians, little is known of what music sounded like at that time. But as two trumpets, one of silver, the other of copper, were found in Tutankhamun's tomb, together with their wooden cores which protected them during travel and storage, it was decided to attempt to play one to see what sound it made. The honour was given to Bandsman Tappern who is shown here about to blow Tutankhamun's silver trumpet into a BBC microphone in 1939. It shattered moments later. But not before a musicologist described its sound as 'raucous and powerful ... recalling rather the timbre of a medieval trombone or primitive horn than that of a trumpet or cornet'. Similar sounds emerged from the copper trumpet which was played without incident in 1939 and 1941. The trumpet on show is the silver one, decorated in gold, which was restored after its explosion.

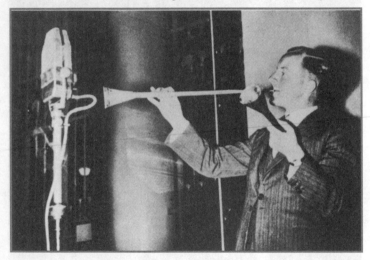

River Boat and Papyrus Boat

Thirty-five model boats were found in Tutankhamun's tomb, some in the annexe, others in the treasury next to the Canopic shrine, as this photograph shows. Two boats are on display in the exhibition: a model of a Nile river boat and a model of a papyrus boat. Both are accurate representations of actual boats of the time. Symbolically the river boat carried Tutankhamun through the hours of the night and in the process offered regeneration. The papyrus boat was to be used for cultic play, for example allowing the king to move about the reeds in his craft in search of hippopotamuses, which represented chaos but were killed by his harpoon.

Cabinet on Long Legs

The entire framework of this elegant cabinet, including the long legs, is made of ebony, while the panels are of a handsome red wood that is probably cedar. Its classical proportions and elaborate decorations make it a very pleasing piece. Also its hieroglyphic inscriptions reveal a great deal about the state of affairs during Tutankhamun's brief reign. Some emphasise his divine nature by calling him the son of Amun who has assigned to him the throne of Geb and the powerful office of Atum – indications of how much the old polytheistic religion had been restored. The central inscription on the lid reads that he is 'beloved of Amun-Ra, king of the gods', yet Aten too is mentioned, and Tutankhamun is called 'the eldest son of Aten in heaven'. Clearly Amun was paramount and Aten was now only one god among many, but the full force of reaction had not yet come, for it was still possible for the king to claim kinship with Aten, whose worship had not yet been proscribed.

Crook and Flail

The crook and the flail were associated with Osiris, lord of the underworld, at a very early date, and it is probable that because the king was considered a son or Horus-figure to Osiris, so the crook and the flail came to signify royal power. Yet while it is not difficult to imagine how the shepherd's crook could have acquired the symbolism of rulership, why the flail should have become associated with Osiris is not so clear. Nevertheless it was the flail which carried the full majesty of royal authority – occasionally a viceroy of Nubia or a vizier might be shown holding a crook, but never the flail. The crook and the flail exhibited here were found lying together in the treasury. The core of the crook is made of copper alloy, while that of the flail is made of wood, but both are coated with dark blue glass which alternates with bands of gold. Another set of the crook and flail were found in the hands of Tutankhamun's outermost mummiform coffin, pictured here.

Making use of the high-tech Computer Topography (CT) scan of Tutankhamun's body undertaken early in 2005, and the skills of paleosculptors, the exhibition will present a **reconstructed bust of the pharaoh** to show what he really looked like on the day he died.

Working from over 1700 high resolution 3-D images, including cross-section views of Tutankhamun's bones, skull and teeth, the two paleographers were able to map the angles and dimensions of the face and transform the raw data into a life-like silicone bust which is meant to reveal the first complete picture of what Tutankhamun really looked like.

The new scanning technique will also be used on other Egyptian mummies. 'CT technology enables us to virtually "unwrap" mummies without damaging them', explains Zahi Hawass, Secretary General of Egypt's Supreme Council of Antiquities.

2. The Search for Tutankhamun

The pyramid-shaped peak of al-Qurn overlooks the remote Valley of the Kings, burial place of Tutankhamun and other 18th Dynasty pharaohs.

Carter, Carnarvon and their quest

A 1920S DETECTIVE STORY IN THE VALLEY OF THE KINGS

The search for Tutankhamun's tomb is a great detective story – one played out against the forbidding backdrop of the **Valley of the Kings** in Upper Egypt – and its discovery by Howard Carter in 1922 remains the most spectacular find in the history of archaeology. Tutankhamun died over 3300 years ago at the age of eighteen or so, and the tomb shows that his burial had been hastily improvised. It was almost miniature by New Kingdom standards, yet its contents take up two wings of the Egyptian Museum in Cairo, its bullion value alone is fabulous, and its artistic value incalculable. Tutankhamun himself remains in his original resting place in the Valley, where over a million visitors a year brave the cauldron heat for a once-in-a-lifetime glimpse of the most famous pharaoh in history.

Howard Carter's pursuit of Tutankhamun was the great object of his life. He had long experience in Egypt, and he knew the Valley of the Kings better than any man alive. Others sometimes thought him foolhardy and obsessed, but Carter's powers of intuition were allied to a trained scientific mind, and armed with nerves of steel against setbacks and disappointments, he was relentless in tracking the boy-king down.

THE MAKING OF AN EGYPTOLOGIST

Howard Carter arrived in Egypt at the age of seventeen, already possessed, as he said, with a 'longing for that country, for the purity of her blue sky, her pale aeriel hills, her valleys teeming with accumulated treasures'. He went there as an artist, and even after he became world famous for the discovery of Tutankhamun's tomb and treasures, he described himself in *Who's Who* as a painter first, an Egyptologist second.

Born in London in 1874, Howard was the youngest son of Samuel John Carter, a successful painter of animals who frequently exhibited at London's Royal Academy. His father sent him to his native Norfolk to be raised by maiden aunts; a sensitive and withdrawn child, he found solace in his own company or close to nature, wandering across the countryside sketching birds and insects. Among Samuel Carter's friends were the Amhersts, wealthy landed gentry who possessed the most important private collection of Egyptian art and papyri in England. When they discovered that Howard, fifteen years old and only just out of school, possessed his father's talent for representing scenes from nature, they employed him as a resident artist at their country home. There, they aroused his fascination with Egypt, giving him the free run of their library and Egyptian galleries.

The Amhersts were also active supporters of the **Egyptian Exploration Fund**, founded in 1882 in order to explore, survey and excavate ancient sites in Egypt and Sudan, and to publish the results. The Fund was at that time excavating among the Middle Kingdom tombs at **Beni Hasan** where an artist was needed to record the decorations on the tomb walls, and through the influence of Lady Amherst the seventeen-year-old Carter was appointed to the job. Within a year he was also serving as apprentice excavator at **Amarna**, site of the heretic pharaoh **Akhenaten**'s capital, under no less a taskmaster than **Sir Flinders Petrie**, one of the most eminent Egyptologists of his day, and then for six years from 1893 he was again copying wall decorations for the Fund, this time at the mortuary temple of **Hatshepsut**, the 18th Dynasty female pharaoh, across the Nile from Luxor at **Deir el Bahri**, not far from the Valley of the Kings. We have engaging glimpses of his pastimes in these years. During the annual inundation, when the Nile overflowed its banks Carter would lie camouflaged with straw on the bottom of a boat and drift across the watery landscape, observing flocks of pelican fishing and feeding. Or he

Howard Carter, left, with Gaston Maspero, the French head of the Egyptian Antiquities Service, during a visit to Carter's work at Thebes in 1913.

would sit with Egyptians in their villages for endless cups of thick black coffee and share in the local gossip, learning their ways and gaining a command of vernacular Arabic unusual among Englishmen in Egypt.

Meanwhile Carter had been noticed by **Gaston Maspero**, Director-General of the Egyptian Antiquities Service, who recognised in him the craftsmanship and integrity of the artist combined with the practical abilities of an excavator and engineer. As Carter's work at Deir el Bahri drew to an end in 1899, Maspero offered him the important and newly created post of Inspector-General of Monuments for Upper Egypt and Nubia, with his headquarters in **Luxor**. The appointment took effect on the first day of the new century, 1 January 1900, when Carter was still only twenty-five years old.

A LONE WOLF IN THE VALLEY OF THE KINGS

Carter never said how or when he had set his heart on finding the tomb of Tutankhamun, but most likely it began around this time, for soon he was building a house on the slope of a hill overlooking the path to the **Valley of the Kings**, the wild and remote burial ground of the **pharaohs of the 18th Dynasty**. Like a lone wolf, Carter wandered among the tombs of the **Theban necropolis** and along the cliffs and into the craggy hills beyond, hardly knowing any human contact, but sensing in the Valley of the Kings a 'religious feeling' so profound 'that it appears almost imbued with a life of its own'.

All this time he filled his notebooks with observations about the tombs and the terrain, and he read extensively among the antique authors and more recent travellers of the eighteenth and nineteenth centuries, anticipating his later reflection that had he not been an archaeologist he would have made a good detective. He knew from the ancient papyri as well as his own explorations that virtually all the **royal tombs of the 18th and 19th Dynasties** had been broken into during the feebler dynasties that followed, and that some of the greatest pharaohs had to be reburied several times. He gathered all his knowledge for his inspectorate report for Maspero in 1903 which detailed everything that was known about all the burial sites of Upper Egypt. Carter came to know the ground, particularly the Valley of the Kings, better probably than anyone alive, and the question always nagging obsessively in his mind was: could any of the kingly tombs have survived intact?

Unlike most of his predecessors, Carter saw **restoration** as part of the task of an Egyptologist, and as Inspector-General he undertook repairs and improvements as far up the Nile as Abu Simbel. He was the first to introduce electric lighting in the Valley of the Kings, banishing flaming torches and dripping candles from the six best royal tombs, making them more accessible, and presenting their decorations to the best effect.

He also began what in effect was his own programme of discovery in the Valley by luring the eccentric American financier **Theodore Davis** into paying for excavations there. Davis had wintered regularly in Egypt since 1889, sailing up and down the Nile in his private *dahabiya* with a lady companion, but now he wanted to have some active antiquarian interest during his sojourns in Upper Egypt. Carter baited him with a conjecture on the whereabouts of the tomb of **Tuthmosis IV**, and said that if Davis would pay for the researches in the Valley of the Kings, the Antiquities Service would allow Carter, his other duties permitting, to conduct the excavations on Davis' behalf.

Early in 1903, after a year of sleuthing in the Valley, Carter discovered the **tomb of Tuthmosis IV**. Alhough it had been looted in ancient times and stripped of all its gold, and although the mummy itself had been removed for safekeeping by the priests to a cache of corpses in the tomb of Amenophis II, the discovery nevertheless yielded a number of valuable objects, including the **faience throwstick**, the **faience figure of the king**, and the **magic brick** that are included in the current Tutankhamun exhibition.

On the back of this success, Carter got Davis to extend his patronage to excavate the **tomb of Hatshepsut**. But the rock was unusually friable, and slithering down the winding passages into the deep and crumbling tomb proved long and dangerous work. For his pains, Carter discovered that the tomb had been vandalised in ancient times and that the roof of its burial chamber had collapsed, though he was able to retrieve Hatshepsut's sarcophagus, now housed in the Cairo Museum. He seems to have been happy enough that this was his last task in the Valley of the Kings before taking up a new appointment early in 1904 as Inspector-General for Lower Egypt, with his headquarters at **Saqqara**, the vast necropolis above Memphis.

Within a year, however, Carter's career was in ruins. A rowdy party of drunken French tourists attempted to visit the Serapeum at Saqqara without buying tickets, and when they were barred from entering, a Frenchman punched one of Carter's Egyptian watchmen in the face, then raised his fist at Carter too. In the ensuing melee, the French threw chairs and stones at Carter and his men, and one of the Frenchmen was knocked down. Returning to Cairo, the French lodged a complaint with their consul, who went to Maspero at the Antiquities Service and demanded that Carter make an apology. Carter replied that it was the French who should apologise. Maspero privately supported Carter but wished to avoid a diplomatic row, and transferred him to a new post in the Delta. Carter felt humiliated, and resigned. That spring he returned to **Luxor** where for the next three years he eked out an existence as a freelance watercolourist, selling his paintings to rich tourists at the **Winter Palace Hotel**.

The gold-plated mask of Tuyu, wife of Yuya and mother of Queen Tiy, is on view in the exhibition. The tomb of Yuya and Tuyu was the most important discovery in the Valley of the Kings until Carter found the tomb of Tutankhamun.

It was an unhappy and frustrating time for Carter, who in February 1906 watched glory pass him by when his successor as Inspector-General at Luxor, **James Quibell**, made a spectacular and unexpected find for Theodore Davis. 'Egypt's Richest Treasure Trove: Wonderful Discoveries in the Valley of the Kings', ran the banner headline in the *Illustrated London News*, describing the barely-disturbed **tomb of Yuya and Tuyu**. Indeed some of the contents of the tomb were so fresh that as Quibell opened a jar to examine its contents, a wasp flew in from outside to sip the still syrupy honey that had been stored away thousands of years ago to nourish Yuya and Tuyu through eternity.

Yuya, who was the commander of the king's cavalry, and his wife **Tuyu** were of common birth, but they were the parents of **Queen Tiy**, the wife of Amenophis III, and they had been – exceptionally – honoured with a burial in the royal valley. Their tomb was filled from ceiling to floor with coffins and funerary equipment, much of it leafed in silver and gold, and all of the finest workmanship that had been found in the Valley to that time. Among the treasures was **Yuya's chariot**, which was remarkably well-preserved, as was the **throne of Princess Sitamun**, their granddaughter who was also a daughter-wife of Amenophis III. The throne was made of wood and partly gilded and plated with silver, its seat cover formed of finely woven string in a herringbone pattern, and its hand rests in the form of gilded female heads, presumably of Sitamun herself. Quibell recalled that when the Empress Eugenie, the elderly widow of Napoleon III, paid a visit to the newly discovered tomb, she looked round for a place to sit, and seeing the throne, said 'Why, there is a chair that will do for me nicely'. Before Quibell's horrified eyes she made herself comfortable on the throne that had not been sat on for over three thousand years. Sitamun's throne and **Tuyu's gilded coffin** and mask as well as a number of other items from the tomb are included in the present exhibition.

HOWARD CARTER (1874–1939)

9 May 1874: Howard Carter is born in London, the youngest son of Samuel John Carter, a successful artist.

1889: Carter works as an artist for the Amherst family, who possess the finest private collection of Egyptian antiquities in England.

1891: Through the influence of Lady Amherst, Carter is sent to Egypt as an artist with the Egypt Exploration Fund.

1892: Carter excavates at Amarna, site of Akhenaten's capital city, under the direction of the great Egyptologist Flinders Petrie.

1893–99: Carter records the wall decorations at Hatshepsut's mortuary temple at Deir el Bahri across the Nile from Luxor.

1900–04: Gaston Maspero, head of the Egyptian Antiquities Service, appoints Carter as the first Inspector-General of Monuments in Upper Egypt and Nubia, with its headquarters in Luxor. Carter encourages Theodore Davis to excavate in the Valley of the Kings, and supervises work on the tombs of Tuthmosis IV and Hatshepsut.

1904: Carter is made Chief Inspector of Antiquities for Lower Egypt, with its headquarters at Saqqara, but is forced to resign the following year after defending his Egyptian workers against French louts.

1905–07: Carter ekes out a living as a watercolourist in Luxor.

1907: Lord Carnarvon employs Carter as his expert excavator at Deir el Bahri on the recommendation of Gaston Maspero.

1914: Carnarvon takes up the concession for excavating at the Valley of the Kings after it is relinquished by Theodore Davis who remarks 'I fear that the Valley of the Tombs is now exhausted'. But with the outbreak of the First World War in August, digging is suspended.

1917–22: The search for Tutankhamun begins in earnest as Carter and Carnarvon resume excavations in the Valley of the Kings.

Summer 1922: Carnarvon decides to abandon excavations, but Carter convinces him to continue for one more season.

4 November 1922: Carter discovers the tomb of Tutankhamun in the Valley of the Kings. The work of clearing the tomb and conserving its treasures will take up the next ten years of Carter's life.

5 April 1923: Lord Carnarvon dies of pneumonia in Cairo following blood poisoning after being bitten by a mosquito at Luxor.

2 March 1939: Howard Carter dies in London.

Davis continued to excavate in the Valley of the Kings until 1914, by when he had discovered or re-examined and cleared thirty-five tombs, pits and caches, so that before relinquishing his concession he felt able to say, 'I fear that the Valley of the Kings is now exhausted.'

LORD CARNARVON ARRIVES IN EGYPT

If fortune played a hand in the discovery of Tutankhamun's tomb, then the occasion was in 1907 when Carter was introduced to the **Fifth Earl of Carnarvon**, an aristocrat and dilettante, who was his complete opposite in almost every way, but who would prove to be his loyal and patient patron for sixteen long and difficult years.

Born in 1866, and therefore eight years older than Carter, Lord Carnarvon was one of the largest and wealthiest landowners in England. At twenty he had sailed round the world, while horse racing, fast motor cars and beautiful women were chief among his many other enthusiasms. But Carnarvon's life as a reckless play-boy was altered by a motoring accident in 1903 which nearly killed him and left him weakened and vulnerable for the rest of his life. On his doctors' orders he wintered in Egypt, but instead of being drawn to the glittering social life of Cairo with its balls, the opera and polo, he made his way to **Luxor**, indulging his newfound enthusiasm for antiquity.

'I may say that at this period I knew nothing whatever about excavating,' Carnarvon wrote of himself later, and the truth is that despite entries in reference books describing him as an 'Egyptologist', he was never more than a happy amateur thrilled at what he might turn up next. But he was also a serious collector and began building up what would eventually become one of the finest private collections of Egyptian antiquities in England. So far as digging was concerned, however, Carnarvon's early methods were so alarming that Gaston Maspero, head of the Antiquities

Service, insisted that he accept the services of an expert excavator, and in 1907 he recommended Howard Carter.

For their first seven years working together, Carnarvon and Carter excavated all along the cliff tops above the **mortuary temples of Hatshepsut, Mentuhotep, Amenophis III, Ramses II and Ramses III**, which stood in the plain of the Theban necropolis on the west side of the Nile. But the results were not encouraging, with Carnarvon writing despairingly of 'open and half-filled mummy pits, heaps of rubbish, great mounds of rock debris with, here and there, fragments of coffins and shreds of linen mummy wrappings protruding from the sand'.

If the ground was yielding few treasures to grow Carnarvon's collection, at least Carter was able to keep his employer happy by obtaining first class antiquities for him on the market. Indeed Carnarvon himself soon acquired a reputation as a connoisseur.

Lord Carnarvon rests on the shaded veranda of Howard Carter's house just outside the Valley of the Kings. Ever since his motoring accident in 1901, Carnarvon had been in less than robust health.

'His taste was faultless and his instinct for the true and genuine was unrivalled,' wrote Sir Wallis Budge of the British Museum about Carnarvon, though as always Carnarvon was acting under the guidance of Carter, a man content to hang back in the shadows, leaving the fame and glamour to shine about the person of his aristocratic patron.

'DEFINITE HOPES OF FINDING THE TOMB OF ONE PARTICULAR KING'

The opportunity Carter and Carnarvon were waiting for came in 1914 when Theodore Davis gave up his concession to excavate in the **Valley of the Kings**. Despite Davis' assertion that the Valley was now exhausted, a view shared by Maspero, Carnarvon followed Carter's urging and obtained the concession for himself. 'There was always the chance that a tomb might reward us in the end,' as Carter put it, adding, 'it was a chance that we were quite willing to take.'

That was the sort of talk that appealed to Carnarvon's gambling spirit, but he also trusted in Carter's intuition and experience, and allowed himself to be guided by his unshakeable self-confidence: 'As a matter of fact we had something more [than a chance]', said Carter. 'I will state that we had definite hopes of finding the tomb of one particular king'.

That king of course was **Tutankhamun**. It was likely, Carter reasoned, that Tutankhamun was buried in the Valley of the Kings. All his predecessors from **Tuthmosis I to Amenophis III** had been buried there, and also Tutankhamun's immediate successors, **Ay** and **Horemheb**. Kings were usually buried in the cemeteries of their capitals, and as Tutankhamun was known to have restored Thebes as the religious capital after Akhenaten had removed it to Amarna, it followed that he would have been buried in the Theban royal valley.

What sealed the matter for Carter was **Davis' discovery in 1908** of a pit containing a dozen large white pottery jars filled with linen, and also bags filled with a dried-out substance, floral collars and other objects. Davis had attached little importance to these, and thinking they were the contents of a small tomb robbed in antiquity, he gave them to the **Metropolitan Museum in New York**. But there they were closely examined and the discovery was made that the dried substance was **natron**, a salt used to desiccate corpses, which along with the linen was left over from the actual embalming of Tutankhamun, while other items were relics of his **funeral banquet** – which took place inside the tomb before it was finally sealed and was attended by eight mourners. When Carter was informed, what had been a probability in his mind became a certainty, that Tutankhamun must be buried in the Valley. But no sooner had Carnarvon obtained the concession to excavate in the Valley of the Kings than the **First World War** broke out in August 1914 and digging was suspended.

During brief intervals in his war-work, acting as a diplomatic messenger and interpreter for the British government in the Middle East, Carter would return to Luxor, and in the spring of 1915, having been made suspicious by some 18th Dynasty objects that had appeared on the market, he investigated the tomb of **Amenophis III**, which had never been properly cleared. When Carter discovered many important pieces of funerary equipment belonging to **Amenophis** and **Queen Tiy**, he took the opportunity to convert Carnarvon's excited interest into a firm commitment to open a full-scale campaign, as soon as circumstances would permit, to find Tutankhamun's tomb in the Valley of the Kings.

THE BARREN YEARS

In December 1917, when Carter and Carnarvon began their search for Tutankhamun in earnest, the difficulty was to know where to begin, for the Valley was covered not only with vast amounts of sand, but also with stone debris from excavations, and nobody had kept a record of which areas had been properly examined and which had not. Carter decided that the only thing to do was to dig right down to bedrock, and he recommended to Carnarvon that they clear the ground within a triangle defined by the **tombs of Ramses II, Merneptah and Ramses VI** – an area which Carter believed had never been touched and where there was a good chance of finding Tutankhamun's tomb. There was no mechanical equipment for clearing, and the large force of labourers employed by Carter used only the traditional adze and basket, so the work went slowly.

The search for the tomb of Tutankhamun went on for seven years and involved removing vast quantities of sand and debris from the floor of the Valley of the Kings.

During their first winter they cleared away a considerable part of the upper layers of the triangle and advanced their excavations right up to the entrance to the tomb of Ramses VI, where they came upon a series of ancient **workmen's huts**. But to excavate in that area would mean cutting off all access to Ramses VI's tomb above, and as it was one of the most popular tombs among tourists to the Valley, they decided to dig elsewhere within the triangle. After six seasons, at a cost of something like half a million dollars a season in today's money, they had removed two hundred thousand tons of sand and rubble but had discovered next to nothing. In obtaining his concession to excavate in the Valley of the Kings, Carnarvon expected that he would be allowed a share of the finds. But he was literally pouring a fortune into the ground and getting very little back. No public organisation would have continued to finance the operation on a show of such meagre results, and though Carter was unshaken, eventually even Lord Carnarvon, wealthy and enlightened enthusiast that he was, concluded that the returns were not commensurate with the cost.

By the summer of 1922 Carnarvon decided to quit, and he invited Carter to **Highclere Castle**, his country home in Berkshire, to discuss the situation. Could there be any justification for continuing with the excavations after all these barren years? But Carter's answer to Carnarvon was that 'so long as a single area of untouched ground remained, the risk was worth taking', and pulling out a map of the Valley, he reminded Carnarvon that there was a small remaining area at the **foot of the approach to the tomb of Ramses VI**. Carter asked for one more season to excavate at that spot, the place where the workmen's huts had been uncovered, and he undertook to bear the costs of the season if it should fail to prove successful. Carnarvon was so touched by Carter's offer that he agreed to a final gamble, only insisting that win or lose the full expense would be Carnarvon's own.

ON THE THRESHOLD OF A MAGNIFICENT DISCOVERY

Carter returned to Egypt in October, and on 1 November 1922 he was back in the Valley of the Kings ready to resume his search for Tutankhamun, this time just below the entrance to the tomb of Ramses VI where he had avoided digging in the winter of 1917–18. On the first day he uncovered the ancient huts erected by the workmen who had constructed Ramses VI's tomb. Patiently he drew plans of them; nothing would go unrecorded before it was cleared away.

On the morning of the fourth day an unusual silence filled the Valley as the workmen stopped tearing at the ground, and Carter immediately knew that something out the ordinary had happened. His workmen had removed the first of the ancient huts and the sand beneath it when suddenly they stopped: they had uncovered a **stone step** cut into the bedrock. Working feverishly that day and the morning of the next, they uncovered step after step, and Carter was now certain that they had found the entrance to a tomb.

But doubt mingled with excitement, for Carter knew from experience that 'there was always the horrible possibility that the tomb was an unfinished one, never completed and never used: if it had been finished there was the depressing probability that it had been completely plundered in ancient times.'

By late afternoon on 4 November, Carter's workmen had uncovered twelve steps, still without reaching the bottom but revealing the upper part of a **doorway**, clearly the entrance to a tunnel cut into the rock. Sunset was approaching and the light was growing dim, but Carter could make out that the doorway, blocked with stones and plastered over, was marked with the impressions of the ancient **necropolis guards** – a recumbent jackal representing the god **Anubis** over the figures of nine foreign captives. 'It was a thrilling moment for an excavator. I found

The entrance to Tutankhamun's tomb (the horizontal rectangle at centre) had been obscured for 3000 years by debris from the construction of the tomb of Ramses VI (the vertical rectangle above).

The sixteen ancient stone steps leading down to the entrance of Tutankhamun's tomb.

Tutankhamun's tomb bore the seal of the necropolis authorities, a jackal and nine captives.

myself, after years of comparatively unproductive labour, on the threshold of what might prove to be a magnificent discovery. Anything, literally anything, might lie beyond.'

On **6 November** Carter sent his famous telegram to Lord Carnarvon: 'At last have made wonderful discovery in the Valley; a magnificent tomb with seals intact; re-covered same for your arrival; congratulations.' While waiting for Carnarvon to travel out from England, Carter ordered his men to refill the excavation to surface level so that it looked as it had before, making the tomb vanish from sight. 'I found it hard to persuade myself at times that the whole episode had not been a dream,' he wrote.

Tutankhamun's Tomb revealed

'WONDERFUL THINGS'

Lord Carnarvon, accompanied by Lady Evelyn Herbert, his 22-year-old daughter, arrived at Luxor on 23 November. On the next day the entire staircase of sixteen steps was cleared, revealing on the lower part of the door the **seal impressions of Tutankhamun**. 'This added enormously to the interest of the discovery,' Carter wrote. 'If we had found, as seemed almost certain, the tomb of that shadowy monarch, whose tenure of the throne coincided with one of the most interesting periods in the whole of Egyptian history, we should indeed have reason to congratulate ourselves.' But it also became apparent that while the Tutankhamun seals appeared on the original plaster, the **Anubis impressions** of the necropolis authorities were used to reseal a portion of the doorway where **robbers** had broken through, probably during the reign of Horemheb.

Nevertheless, Carter and Carnarvon consoled themselves with the thought that the authorities would not have resealed the tomb had there not been something worthwhile to protect. After the seals were photographed, they were removed, the door was opened, and a descending passage was revealed, nearly seven feet high. This was filled with stones and rubble, again showing evidence of restoration after penetration by thieves. Thirty feet along this passage was a second doorway, likewise bearing the seal impressions of Tutankhamun and of the necropolis authorities.

By 26 November everything was ready to take down the blocks of stone filling the **second doorway**. With Lady Evelyn, Lord Carnarvon and his assistant Arthur Callender standing beside him, Carter prised out some of the stones and inserted a candle through the hole: 'At first I could see nothing, the hot air escaping from the chamber causing the candle to flicker, but presently, as my eyes grew accustomed to the light, details of the room within emerged slowly from the mist, strange animals, statues, and gold – everywhere the glint of gold. For the moment – an eternity it must have seemed to the others standing by – I was struck dumb with amazement, and when Lord Carnarvon, unable to stand the suspense any longer, inquired anxiously "Can you see anything?" it was all I could do to get out the words "Yes, wonderful things."'

Carter was gazing into the **antechamber**. 'Surely never before in the whole history of excavation had such an amazing sight been seen as the light of our [electric] torch revealed to us.' For Carter,

The antechamber of Tutankhamun's tomb when it was first glimpsed by Howard Carter and Lord Carnarvon in November 1922.

November 26 1922 was 'the day of days, the most wonderful that I have ever lived through, and certainly one whose like I can never hope to see again'. What he saw convinced him that the robbers had made little inroad and that the find would exceed his wildest dreams. Among the plethora of objects were statues large and small, treasure-filled chests of all sizes, a chariot and thrones, as well as several items included in the current exhibition: the small **gold-leafed statue shrine** adorned with charming incised scenes of the king with his young wife Ankhesenamun; the **crook with a handle** in the form of a Nubian captive; and the **mannequin of Tutankhamun** himself.

SECRET RETURN TO THE TOMB

Carter, Carnarvon, Evelyn and Callender in fact lived through 26 November not once but twice, for they secretly returned to the tomb that night, or possibly on the night of 28 November, before its official opening on the 29th. Nor did they merely peer into the antechamber through a hole in the second doorway: they entered the antechamber itself, and also broke into the burial chamber of Tutankhamun (which Carter claimed not to have entered until three months later). Carter's wonderfully atmospheric description of their first glimpse into the tomb is even more dramatic when you know that really all four of them had penetrated deep into the tomb and wandered about amid the ghosts of another time.

'I suppose most excavators would confess to a feeling of awe – embarrassment almost – when they break into a chamber closed and sealed by pious hands so many centuries ago. For the moment, time as a factor in human life has lost its meaning. Three thousand, four thousand years maybe, have passed and gone since human feet last trod the floor on which you stand, and yet, as you note the signs of recent life around you – the half-filled bowl of mortar for the door, the blackened lamp, the

Lifesize ka statues of Tutankhamun stand as guardians on either side of the doorway leading into the burial chamber of his tomb. Carter has removed most of the blocking from the doorway, revealing the golden shrine within.

finger-mark upon the freshly painted surface, the farewell garland dropped upon the threshold – you feel it might have been but yesterday. The very air you breathe, unchanged throughout centuries, you share with those who laid the mummy to its rest. Time is annihilated by little intimate details such as these, and you feel an intruder.

'That is perhaps the first and dominant sensation, but others follow thick and fast – the exhilaration of discovery, the fever of suspense, the almost over-mastering impulse, born of curiosity, to break down seals and lift the lids of boxes, the thought – pure joy to the investigator – that you are about to add a page to history, or solve some problem of research, the strained expectancy – why not confess it? – of the treasure-seeker.'

Carter and his companions were entirely within their rights to enter the various chambers of the tomb at any time they liked, but their secret entry, when it was found out decades later, prompted speculation about Carter's integrity. However, the reason for their secret entry is understandable enough; signs that the tomb had been entered in the ancient past roused fears that its holy of holies, the burial chamber itself, had been plundered.

In fact, back in 1900 when Carter discovered the tomb of the Middle Kingdom pharaoh Mentuhotep II in the Theban necropolis outside the Valley of the Kings, the highest dignitaries were invited to witness him breaking down the wall into the burial chamber. Gaston Maspero was there along with the Egyptian prime minister and the British consul general, all of them sweltering as they waited 300 feet below the ground. 'I had everything prepared,' Carter wrote in his notebook. 'The long wished for moment had arrived. We were ready to penetrate the mystery

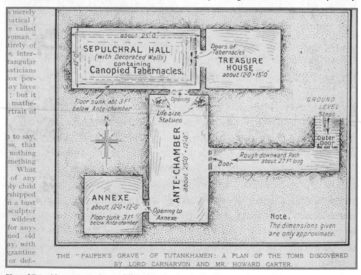

Plan of Tutankhamun's tomb as published at the time in the Illustrated London News. What appears here as the sepulchral hall with its canopied tabernacles is the burial chamber with its sarcophagus enclosed by golden shrines.

behind the masonry. I removed the heavy limestone slabs, block by block. The door was at last open. It led directly into a small room which was partially filled with rock chips, just as the Egyptian masons had left it, but it was otherwise empty save for some pottery water jars and some pieces of wood. At first glance I felt that there must be another doorway leading to another chamber, but a cursory examination proved that there was nothing of the sort. I was filled with dismay.'

That last remark was an understatement; Carter looked like a complete fool. Now at the tomb of Tutankhamun he had no intention of looking like a fool again. And so before turning to the task of methodically photographing and describing every object in the antechamber, Carter could not resist knowing what lay behind the blocked up door beyond, indeed knowing how much farther the tomb extended. His anxiety was all the greater as the **door to the burial chamber**, like the outermost door to the tomb itself, showed evidence of having been resealed. Carter discovered that thieves had indeed broken into the burial chamber, but they had been stopped before they could reach the mummy.

This meant that for the first time it was possible to see **how a pharaoh was buried**. Many mummies of Egyptian kings had been found before, but only Amenophis II was in his original tomb, and all the valuables buried with him had been robbed. But in the case of Tutankhamun not only his mummy but his coffins and all the treasures they enclosed were found intact, as well as the vast amount of funerary equipment within the chambers of the tomb.

CLEARING THE TOMB

Carter's clearance task was enormous – more than could be accomplished by himself and his assistant Arthur Callender. The burial chamber could not properly be examined without removing most of the objects from the anteroom, and in any case everything had to be scientifically recorded and photographed, with many items needing restoring before they could be removed from the tomb.

In December help was offered from various quarters, and Carter picked his team well. **Dr Alan Gardiner** and **Professor Percy Newberry** undertook to record the **hieroglyphics**, and **Alfred Lucas**, Director of the Chemical Department of the Egyptian Government, who set up his field laboratory in the tomb of Seti II, was made responsible for giving **scientific advice** on moving objects from the tomb and for the conservation of many weak pieces, so that their safe arrival at the Egyptian Museum in Cairo would be assured. Also the **Metropolitan Museum in New York** lent Carter the help of two draughtsmen, as well as the assistance of two Englishmen in its employ, the archaeologist **Arthur Mace** and the photographer **Harry Burton**.

In all it took from **1922 until 1932** for Carter's team to complete their arduous and meticulous task, which proved a model of its kind. After restoring, recording and packing each object in the sweltering tomb or in the frying pan atmosphere of the Valley of the Kings, they then had to transport them over five and a half miles of rugged terrain to the banks of the Nile. For this, Carter improvised a hand-laid railway from a few lengths of track, which required that after the trucks loaded with the packing crates had been pushed over them the rails had to be lifted and relaid farther forward. With a gang of fifty men managing a rate of a third of a mile an hour, each journey took fifteen hours, and this in the fiery heat of the sun when the iron rails were almost too hot to touch. And if the heat was not enough, Carter also had to contend with the intrusions and demands of thousands of tourists and an hysterical press, for the discovery of Tutankhamun's tomb was the biggest story in the world, and Carter and Carnarvon had been transformed overnight into celebrities. Finally the crates were loaded onto a steam vessel and seven days later were delivered safely to the museum in Cairo. As has been generally agreed by

Callender and Carter carefully wrap the guardian figure of Tutankhamun before removing it from the tomb. Only after clearing the antechamber will it be possible to properly investigate the burial chamber beyond.

Carter leads his workmen as they carry the mannequin of Tutankhamun out of the Valley of the Kings to the Nile where a steamer will transport it to the Egyptian Museum in Cairo.

archaeologists and historians since, had the tomb been found by anyone other than Howard Carter, it would have been cleared not in ten years but in ten days, with any surviving artefacts put on display within a month.

'PRESENT AT THE FUNERAL OF A KING LONG DEAD'

On 17 February 1923, three months after the secret entry, Carter staged the official **opening of the burial chamber**. With the assistance of Callender and Mace, and in the presence of Carnarvon and his daughter Lady Evelyn, and an assemblage of archaeologists and Egyptian dignitaries, Carter removed stone after stone from the sealed door. Behind it rose what seemed to be a wall of solid gold – in fact the side of the immense gilt shrine built to cover and protect the sarcophagus.

The Times of London reported the events as follows:

This has perhaps been the most extraordinary day in the whole history of Egyptian excavation. Whatever anyone may have guessed or imagined of the secret of Tutankhamun's tomb, they surely cannot have dreamed the truth as now revealed. Entrance today was made into the sealed chamber, and yet another door opened beyond that. No eyes have yet seen the King, but to a practical certainty, we now know that he lies there, close at hand, in all his original state undisturbed.

Moreover, in addition to the great store of treasures, which the tomb has already yielded, to-day has bought to light a new wealth of objects of artistic, historical, and even intrinsic value which is bewildering. It is such a hoard as the most sanguine excavator can hardly have pictured even in visions in his sleep, and puts Lord Carnarvon's and Mr. Carter's discovery in a class by itself above all previous finds.

The process of opening the doorway bearing the Royal insignia and guarded by protective statues of the King had taken several hours of careful manipulation under intense heat. It finally ended in a wonderful revelation, for before the spectators was the resplendent mausoleum of the King, a spacious beautiful, decorated chamber, completely occupied by an immense shrine covered with gold inlaid with brilliant blue faience.

Having cleared the antechamber, Carter removes the entire wall dividing it from the burial chamber to give him comfortable access to the golden shrines within.

This beautiful wooden construction towers nearly to the ceiling and fills the great sepulchral hall within a short span of its four walls. Its sides are adorned with magnificent religious texts and fearful symbols of the dead, and it is capped with a superb cornice and torus moulding.

The foregoing narrative is necessarily hasty, and may be subject to correction in details as the result of future investigation.

Watching the visitors, led by Carnarvon, enter and then emerge from the burial chamber, Carter described how 'each had a dazed, bewildered look in his eyes, and each in turn, as he came out, threw up his hands before him, an unconscious gesture of impotence to describe in words the wonders that he had seen. In imagination – and not wholly in imagination either – we had been present at the funeral ceremonies of a king long dead and almost forgotten. At a quarter past two we had filed down into the tomb, and when, three hours later, hot, dusty, and dishevelled, we came out once more into the light of day, the very Valley seemed to have changed for us and taken on a more personal aspect. We had been given the Freedom.'

Seven weeks later, before the golden shrine was dismantled and Tutankhamun's sarcophagus revealed, Lord Carnarvon was dead.

The Curse of Tutankhamun

AND THE STRANGE CASE OF CARTER'S CANARY

When Carter returned to Egypt in the autumn of 1922 for his last-ditch attempt to find Tutankhamun's tomb, he brought with him from England a **canary**, which he kept in a cage outside his house near the entrance to the Valley of the Kings. People came from near and far to hear it sing, for there were no songbirds in that part of Egypt, and they had heard nothing like it before.

'The bird will bring good fortune,' they all agreed, while Carter himself felt it seemed to share his own moods. He noticed that it was chirping especially merrily on the morning of 6 November when he went to the Luxor telegraph office to send his famous cable to Carnarvon. Later that day when he went to the Valley of the Kings he learnt that his workmen had adopted his canary as a talisman and had named his great discovery the 'Tomb of the Bird'. But not long after Carter's and Carnarvon's official entry into Tutankhamun's burial chamber in February 1923, a strange incident occurred, which was noted by the American Egyptologist James Henry Breasted, who was visiting at the time.

Carter had sent one of his men on an errand to his house, but on nearing it the man thought he heard a 'faint, almost human cry'. Reaching the house, he looked up at the cage hanging near the entrance: coiled up within it was a cobra, the ancient

Howard Carter stares across 3000 years of time as he pears through the doors of the four gilded shrines enclosing the sarcophagus of Tutankhamun.

Egyptian symbol of royal power, and in its mouth was Carter's dead canary. The news spread rapidly to Luxor and through the Valley of the Kings, where people took it as a sign of the dead king's anger at the violation of his tomb. 'Now something terrible will happen,' they said. Within six months of the find, Carnarvon was dead, Carter was close to a nervous breakdown, and the face of Egyptology was changed forever.

TENSIONS BETWEEN CARTER AND CARNARVON

The discovery of Tutankhamun's tomb had turned Carter and his aristocratic patron into the most famous men in the world. Telegrams poured in from every quarter of the globe, then letters by the bag-full, while droves of journalists from every newspaper worthy of the name descended on the Valley, followed by so many tourists that Luxor's hotels had to erect tents for them in their gardens. 'Archaeology under the limelight is a new and rather bewildering experience for most of us', Carter reflected. 'In the past we have gone about our business happily enough, intensely interested in it ourselves, but not expecting other folk to be more than tepidly polite about it, and now all of a sudden we find the world takes an interest in us, an interest so intense and so avid for details that special correspondents at large salaries have to be sent to interview us, report our every movement, and hide round corners to surprise a secret out of us.'

Carnarvon, who went back to England in December before returning to Luxor in February for the official opening of Tutankhamun's burial chamber, was as comfortable with his new-found celebrity as he was removed from the day-to-day pressures of the work. But Carter, who bore direct responsibility for record-ing, preserving and clearing the contents of the tomb, was con-tinually being diverted from the job at hand by the importuning of the press and public. The work of the archaeologist was as seri-ous as that of the chemist in his laboratory or the surgeon carry-

ing out an operation, he argued, and no one would think of inter-
rupting them. But in the public mind, he said, 'archaeology is not
work at all. Excavation is a sort of super-tourist amusement.'

The problem of **press harassment** looked like being solved by
Carnarvon's exclusivity agreement with **The Times** of London,
which earned him a cash payment of half a million dollars in
today's money plus 75 percent of all profits from the syndication of
articles and photographs to other newspapers and magazines.
Though there was no financial benefit for Carter in the arrangement, he favoured the agreement with *The Times* because it would
ensure accurate reporting, and because in theory it meant he had to
deal with only one newspaper and not the scores of journalists
crawling all over Luxor and the Valley of the Kings. But in striking
a deal with a single newspaper, Carnarvon made an enemy of the
rest of the world's press, who resented being shut out from the
biggest story of the age. As a journalist working for *The New York
Times* put it, he would 'drive C and C out of their minds for having sold a piece of the world's ancient history to the London *Times*'.

Against this difficult background, and especially after their official entry into the burial chamber on 17 February, things began
to go wrong between Carter and Carnarvon. 'The man is by no
means wholly to blame,' was Breasted's view of Carter. 'What he
has gone through has broken him down.' Tension grew between
Carter and Carnarvon, and soon irritation turned into antago-
nism, until on 26 February, after a blazing row, Carter closed the
tomb. 'This made a complete break,' he explained, as it put a final
stop to the unceasing interruptions to his work by journalists and
tourists. Perhaps it was only that: the pressures and frustrations
had momentarily become too much. But he did not stop with the
tomb; the break was with Carnarvon too. Early in March, when
Carnarvon came round to try and make things up, more bitter
words were exchanged and Carter ordered his friend and patron
from his house, telling him never to return.

Lord Carnarvon and his daughter Evelyn with Carter at the entrance to the tomb. Some think that an unspoken love between Evelyn and Carter was the cause of the row between the two men.

Romantics have surmised that **Lady Evelyn**, Carnarvon's beautiful young daughter, was the cause of their dispute. They point to a note that Carnarvon sent to Carter early on in their quarrel, saying, 'I have been feeling very unhappy today. I did not know what to think or to do and when I saw Eve she told me everything.' Had Evelyn and Carter become emotionally involved? She was the apple of her father's eye and he would have been highly protective of her. Did Carnarvon object to a relationship with a man twice her age? Did Carter insensitively brush Evelyn aside? But the 'everything' that Evelyn told her father need not have concerned herself and Carter at all, and more likely she was simply playing the role of a peacemaker and carrying messages between the two.

Or possibly the argument was over the **distribution of the finds**. The terms of Carnarvon's concession to excavate in the Valley of the

Kings specified that all mummies of kings, princes and high officials were the property of the state, and that the contents of intact tombs must be handed over to the **Egyptian Museum in Cairo**. But in the case of tombs robbed in antiquity, the excavator would be entitled to a share which would sufficiently recompense him for the undertaking. Carnarvon therefore anticipated receiving a large portion of the tomb's contents. However, the discovery of Tutankhamun's tomb was exciting nationalist feelings and the Egyptian government was under pressure to revise the rules. Carter, according to Breasted, urged Carnarvon to renounce any rights or claims to the contents of the tomb. But Carnarvon, who was a collector first and foremost and had spent the equivalent in today's terms of well over three million dollars on searching for Tutankhamun in the Valley of the Kings, was now looking for a return on his years of investment.

But whatever the external factors, there must also have been the altered relationship between the two men, for in the triumph of his discovery Carter was emerging from the patronage of Carnarvon. And though a sensitive man, Carter was a socially awkward figure, seemingly without feelings and lacking in diplomatic skills. Perhaps the envy of the years combined with the stresses of the moment caused Carter to speak bitterly and woundingly to his old friend. Carnarvon sent a note to Carter at this time, saying, 'I have done many foolish things and I am very sorry. But there is only one thing I want to say to you which I hope you will always remember – whatever your feelings are or will be for me in the future my affection for you will never change.'

THE DEATH OF LORD CARNARVON

Just after the final row with Carter early in March, **Carnarvon** was bitten on his cheek by a **mosquito**. Then while shaving in his suite at Luxor's Winter Palace Hotel, he cut into the swelling, which became infected. Running a high fever and worn out by recent events, Carnarvon was ordered to bed by a doctor. Looked after by his daughter, he seemed, after two days' rest, to have recovered, and was eager to visit the tomb. But almost immediately he suffered a relapse. Receiving news from Evelyn that Carnarvon would be taken to Cairo, Carter at once called at the Winter Palace where the two friends shook hands and were reconciled. Though only 57, Carnarvon had been a weakened man since his motoring accident twenty years before, and in the days before penicillin he was an easy prey to infection, which by 26 March had developed into blood poisoning. Pneumonia set in, and finally on 5 April 1923 *The Times* reported from Cairo, 'Lord Carnarvon died peacefully this morning at 2 o'clock. He was conscious almost to the end.'

Strange events were reported in the more sensational newspapers. The lights went out in Cairo at the very instant, it was said, of Carnarvon's death, while a thousand miles away at Highclere Castle Carnarvon's dog Susie howled inconsolably and died within minutes of her master. Soon the **'Curse of Tutankhamun'** was spotted everywhere, though for the most part its origins can be traced to newspaper offices around the world. When Carnarvon sold exclusive coverage of the tomb story, including photographs, to *The Times*, he left other newspapers empty-handed. And, as newspapers will, they simply invented a story of their own.

Popular novelists joined in, among them **Arthur Conan Doyle**, the creator of Sherlock Holmes, who attributed Carnarvon's death to 'elementals – not souls, not spirits – created by Tutankhamun's priests to guard the tomb'. But unlike his famous detective, Conan Doyle was far from possessing a rational personality and was notorious for his interest in the occult, and in particular for believing in garden fairies.

Furthermore there was something of a **literary tradition** in **curses from the mummy's tomb**, traceable not to ancient Egypt but to early nineteenth-century England. A show held near Piccadilly Circus in 1821 in which mummies were unwrapped

MOST FAMOUS OF DISCOVERERS IN EGYPT: A TRAGIC DEATH.

The death of Lord Carnarvon is announced in the Illustrated London News. For the sake of a good story that would run and run, journalists claimed that Carnarvon had been struck down by the curse of Tutankhamun.

inspired the novelist Jane Loudon Webb to write a shocker called *The Mummy*, which involved a bookish Egyptologist called Edric being stalked by the eponymous corpse. Later Louisa May Alcott, the author of *Little Women*, pursued the idea in a short story called *The Mummy's Curse*. The press was in fact recycling old news, and Hollywood was not long to follow.

FACE TO FACE WITH TUTANKHAMUN

After consulting with Howard Carter, and determined to continue with what he and her husband had begun, Lady Carnarvon renewed the concession to dig at the Valley of the Kings. In October 1923, six months after Carnarvon's death, Carter resumed work at the tomb, patiently disassembling the golden shrines inside the burial

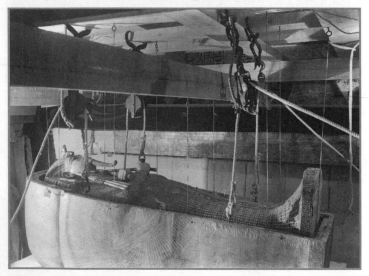

With enormous difficulty and ingenuity within the confined space of the burial chamber, Carter raised the heavy stone lid from the massive quartzite sarcophagus of Tutankhamun.

chamber. Carter estimated that the task would take a month, but crowds of journalists and sightseers round the tomb were bringing his work nearly to a standstill, so that it was not until February 1924 that the great quartzite **sarcophagus** stood revealed. Before a selected group of archaeologists and Egyptian officials, whom Carter invited on February 12th, he gave the order for the system of ropes and pulleys to lift the sarcophagus lid.

'Amid intense silence', as Carter described the scene, 'the huge slab weighing over a ton and a quarter, rose from its bed.' A veil of linen shrouds obscured what lay within, and Carter rolled these back one by one. 'As the last was removed a gasp of wonderment escaped our lips, so gorgeous was the sight that met our eyes: a golden effigy of the young boy-king, of most magnificent workmanship, filled the whole of the sarcophagus.

One by one, Carter removed the veil of linen shrouds from the gold coffin, revealing the features of the king. A wreath of flowers had been placed upon his forehead over 3000 years before.

85

'Upon the forehead of this recumbent figure of the young boy-king were two emblems delicately worked in brilliant inlay – the cobra and the vulture – symbols of Upper and Lower Egypt, but perhaps the most touching by its human simplicity was the tiny wreath of flowers around these symbols, as it pleased us to think, the last farewell offering of the widowed girl queen to her husband.'

'Among all that regal splendour, that royal magnificence – everywhere the glint of gold – there was nothing so beautiful as those few withered flowers, still retaining their tinge of colour. They told us what a short period three thousand three hundred years really was – but Yesterday and the Morrow.'

TUTANKHAMUN AND EGYPTIAN NATIONALISM

On the following day, 13 February, Carter wanted to make a personal gesture of thanks by inviting the wives and families of his archaeological team and his senior Egyptian workers to a guided tour of Tutankhamun's tomb. But that morning he received a message from the **Minister of Public Works**, forbidding him from doing so. It was an assertion of Egyptian claims over those of Carter, in his capacity as representative of Lady Carnarvon, and its arrogance outraged him.

Supported by every eminent archaeologist in Egypt at the time, Carter signed a notice that had been agreed among them and posted it in the lobby of the Winter Palace Hotel that same afternoon: 'Owing to the impossible restrictions and discourtesies on the part of the Public Works Department and its Antiquities Service all my collaborators in protest have refused to work any further upon the scientific investigation of the discovery of the tomb of Tutankhamun' – at which Carter closed and padlocked the tomb, announcing that no further work could be carried out.

Carter welcomes a party of Egyptians to the tomb after the nationalists' political row had subsided. The large man at the centre is King Fuad, and behind his right shoulder is the royal chamberlain Ahmed Hassanein Bey.

But Carter had made a serious mistake. The days were now over when Egyptology was a loosely regulated archaeological Klondike in which foreign excavators were granted concessions that gave them rights over access and to a share of what they found (not without justice, as the expertise and cost were theirs and also the historical interest). The Egyptians themselves had been largely incurious about the past. The discovery of Tutankhamun's tomb coincided with the swell of **Egyptian nationalism** that followed the First World War, and the Cairo government soon spotted the long arm of British imperialism snatching at the country's ancient heritage. With the affable, glamorous Carnarvon gone, the brusque and awkward Carter was easily portrayed as the downside of colonialism, and in the question of finder's versus Egyptian rights, Carter found himself cast in the role of an imperialist villain. His closure of the tomb allowed the Egyptian government to declare that he had abandoned his responsibilities and violated the terms of the concession, and it confiscated the tomb along with all its contents.

Unwisely, Carter took **legal action** to re-establish the Carnarvon claim, but succeeded only in heaping obloquy on himself. However, once the sovereign rights of the state were upheld in the courts, and the Egyptian government was confident that it had the upper hand, it agreed a compromise with all the parties. Lady Carnarvon was obliged to surrender any claim to the treasures of Tutankhamun – which ironically is what Carter had wanted in the first place – and in return was compensated virtually in full for the sums Lord Carnarvon had spent in searching for and excavating the tomb. Carter was granted a **new concession** in his own name, his work to be financed by the Egyptians and from his own pocket.

Yet despite the satisfactory ending from an archaeological point of view, the Tutankhamun controversy had been a political embarrassment to Carter's compatriots, and it is notable that his country never honoured him for his achievement.

'DEATH SHALL COME ON SWIFT WINGS'

An inscription supposedly found in Tutankhamun's tomb, though in fact the invention of a journalist, read, 'Death shall come on swift wings to him who disturbs the peace of the king.' But was there a curse?

'Tommy-rot', was always Carter's irritated reply. And in so far as the curse was meant to apply to the lives of those associated with the discovery of the tomb, Carter was right. The press would claim that twenty-six people connected with the find died within a decade. In fact, even ten years later only one of the five people present at the tomb's opening had died – and that was Lord Carnarvon, who since his motoring accident twenty years earlier had been a sick and weakened man. There were only two further deaths among the twenty-two people who witnessed the opening of the sarcophagus; and of the ten who were present at the

The principal members of Carter's team take a break for lunch in the tomb of Ramses XI in 1923. From left to right they are Breasted, Burton, Lucas, Callender (at the head of the table), Mace, Carter and Gardiner. Carnarvon, who took the picture, died soon after, and Mace died in 1928.

unwrapping of the mummy, none had died at all. Several of the chief figures in the excavation died in their sixties, while many lived well into their eighties.

Carter himself died at the age of sixty-five. The clearance of the tomb had taken him and his helpers ten years, and he was in poor health for the latter part of his work. As a result he was unable to write a scientific publication of the material that he had brought to light, though he did write a brilliant popular account in three volumes, the first volume with A.C. Mace. He died seven years later, in London in 1939.

Tutankhamun's Tomb today

Not surprisingly, Tutankhamun's tomb remains one of the key attractions for visitors to Egypt. It only takes a little imagination to conjure up Carter and Carnavon's glimpse of 'wonderful things' – and, of course, you can see most of those things in the Egyptian Museum at Cairo. The contents of the current touring exhibition are just a tiny portion – albeit a beautiful one – of the tomb's finds.

TUTANKHAMUN'S TOMB

A short descending corridor leads to the **antechamber** in which Carter and Carnarvon had their first glimpse of the treasures through the blocked-up doorway. Among these hundreds of pieces were four **royal chariots**, three **ritual couches**, the **mannequin of Tutankhamun** and the two lifesize figures of **guardians** in the form of the king.

Off the **antechamber** is the **annexe**, now walled up, which contained all sorts of **provisions** for the afterlife, including unguents, oils and jars of red wine, as well as stools, chairs, bedsteads and storage boxes. The two **guardian figures** at the far end of the antechamber stood on either side of another blocked-up doorway sealing off the burial chamber, which was almost entire-

91

The east wall (top) of the burial chamber shows the mummified Tutankhamun being transported on a sledge. The north wall (bottom) depicts the opening of the mouth ceremony performed by Ay on the right.

On the south wall (top) Tutankhamun is welcomed into the afterworld by Hathor and the jackal-headed Anubis. On the west wall (bottom) a scarab representing the sun navigates aboard his solar boat through the hours of darkness symbolised by the twelve baboons.

ly filled with the four **gilded shrines** erected round the quartzite sarcophagus containing two gilded wooden coffins and the innermost solid gold anthropoid coffin weighing nearly 250 lbs (110.4 kilograms). In this lay the **mummy** of Tutankhamun, his body bedecked with jewellery and his head covered by a gold mask. Today the entire wall between the antechamber and the burial chamber has been removed and replaced with a railing; visitors cannot go beyond this point.

This is the only **decorated chamber** in the tomb, its paintings a hasty abbreviation of the extensive funerary décor of grander tombs in the Valley. On the **east wall** the mummified king, placed within a shrine, is transported on a sledge. On the **north wall**, from right to left, Ay performs the opening of the mouth ceremony, traditionally the role of a king's son, on Tutankhamun who is depicted in the form of Osiris, lord of the underworld; Tutankhamun is greeted by the goddess Nut; and Tutankhamun is welcomed to the underworld by Osiris. The **south wall** (almost impossible to see from the railing) continues the theme of the north wall, and again Tutankhamun is shown being welcomed to the underworld, Hathor standing in front of him, and behind him jackal-headed Anubis. The **west wall** is decorated with an extract from the Amduat, a sacred text for navigating through the night before being reborn with the sun at dawn. The baboons represent the twelve hours of darkness, while the scarab represents the sun voyaging on the solar boat.

The **treasury** opens off to one side of the burial chamber and among its welter of objects contained the **Anubis shrine** surmounted by a jackal; the gilded **canopic shrine** enclosing the alabaster box and jars containing the king's viscera; and the **embalmed foetuses** of Tutankhamun's still-born children by his young wife Ankhesenamum. As for **Tutankhamun himself**, his body has been returned to the burial chamber, where it lies within the outermost of his three coffins, inside his sarcophagus.

THE TREASURES ON DISPLAY

That one coffin apart, Tutankhamun lies in his tomb alone, for virtually everything else has been removed from the various chambers and put on open display. A few fine and interesting objects are housed at the **Museum of Ancient Egyptian Art in Luxor**, but the great bulk are at the **Egyptian Museum in Cairo**. Here the 1700-odd objects from Tutankhamun's tomb take up two galleries.

Most of the objects found in the tomb are without parallel, so it is difficult to know how they compared in quality with the burial goods and funerary equipment of other pharaohs, though in

The golden mask of Tutankhamun is on public display at the Egyptian Museum in Cairo, but to visit the boy king himself you must go to his tomb in the Valley of the Kings.

the few instances where comparison is possible, the artefacts found in the tomb are far richer and finer. Many display a level of workmanship and technical skill which is almost unbelievable, and indeed many are works of art which bear comparison with the finest products of the ancient world.

Nearby in the museum are the contents from the tomb of **Yuya and Tuyu**, also statues of **Amenophis III** and **Queen Tiy**, and of **Akhenaten** and **Nefertiti**, along with many other artefacts associated with them. Together with the treasures of Tutankhamun, these take up a good third of the whole museum, which speaks of the richness of the 18th Dynasty, and especially of those three or four generations which Tutankhamun would have known as his immediate family. Although the 130 pieces in the present exhibition, *Tutankhamun and the Golden Age of the Pharaohs*, are only a small proportion of the abundant finds made by Howard Carter and others in the Valley of the Kings, they include many of the family's finest treasures.

3. The 18th Dynasty

The Historical Context of Tutankhamun

The Hypostyle Hall in the temple of Amun at Karnak.

The 18th Dynasty

Tutankhamun was the last pharaoh in the bloodline of the remarkable **18th Dynasty** – the kings and queens who ruled over Egypt during one of the most magnificent and dramatic epochs in its history. Indeed, when we think of ancient Egypt, of its opulence and grandeur, its colossal monuments and statues, and its treasure-filled tombs, we are thinking mostly of that period called the **New Kingdom** which was inaugurated by Tutankhamun's ancestors, those warrior kings who liberated Egypt from a foreign occupier and went on to create the world's first empire.

Though the 18th Dynasty ruled for hardly more than 250 years, from **1550 BC to 1295 BC**, it was a momentous time for Egypt. Its kings transformed their capital of **Thebes** into the greatest city in the ancient world. Wealthy and cosmopolitan, Thebes' cultural and mercantile relations extended throughout the Eastern Mediterranean, and its military power reached deep into Africa along the upwaters of the Nile, and far across the Near East beyond the banks of the Euphrates river. This section tells the story of this glorious age, which reached its apogee during the reign of Amenophis III. But also there is another story to tell, of the great **upheaval in religious belief** which followed.

A major beneficiary of imperial wealth was the priesthood of the **god Amun** at the great temple of **Karnak** at Thebes. Attempts to limit its power, which rivalled that of the pharaohs, came to a head during the reign of **Akhenaten**, who was probably Tutankhamun's father. Turning against ancient Egypt's traditional polytheistic religion, Akhenaten introduced the **worship of Aten**, whom he proclaimed as the one and only god – the first appearance in history of monotheism. It was Tutankhamun who began the counter-revolution, reasserting the old gods.

CHRONOLOGY (ALL DATES BC)

Early Dynastic Period	
1st–2nd dynasties	c.3000–2686

Old Kingdom	
3rd–8th dynasties	2686–2125

First Intermediate Period	
9th–11th dynasties	2160–2055

Middle Kingdom	
12th–14th dynasties	2055–1650

Second Intermediate Period	
15th–17th dynasties	1650–1550

New Kingdom	
18th Dynasty	1550–1307
Amosis	1550–1525
Amenophis I	1525–1504
Tuthmosis I	1504–1492
Tuthmosis II	1492–1479
Tuthmosis III	1479–1425
Hatshepsut	1473–1458
Amenophis II	1427–1400
Tuthmosis IV	1400–1390
Amenophis III	1390–1352
Amenophis IV/Akhenaten	1352–1336
Smenkhkare (Nefertiti)	1338–1336
Tutankhamun	1336–1327
Ay	1327–1323
Horemheb	1323–1295

New Kingdom contd.	
19th Dynasty	1295–1186
Ramses I	1295–1294
Seti I	1294–1279
Ramses II	1279–1213
Merneptah	1213–1203
Seti II	1203–1194
Siptah	1194–1188
Twosre	1188–1186
20th Dynasty	1186–1069
Sethnekht	1186–1184
Ramses III	1184–1153
Ramses IV	1153–1150
Ramses V	1150–1147
Ramses VI	1147–1143
Ramses VII	1143–1136
Ramses VIII	1136–1131
Ramses IX	1131–1112
Ramses X	1112–1100
Ramses XI	1100–1069

Third Intermediate Period	
21st–25th Dynasties	1069–664

Late Period	
25th Dynasty–2nd Persian Period	664–332

Graeco-Roman Period	
Ptolemic Dynasty-Roman Emperors	332 BC–AD 395

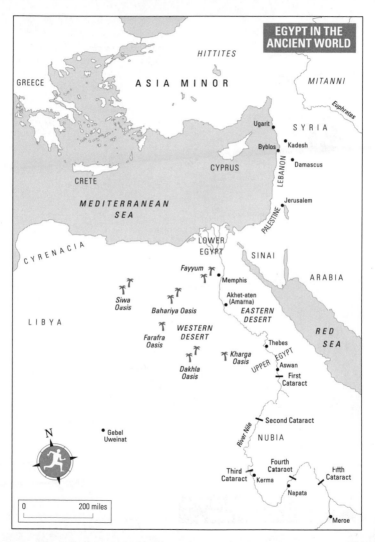

EGYPT IN THE ANCIENT WORLD

HITTITES

GREECE

ASIA MINOR

MITANNI

Euphrates

Ugarit

SYRIA

Byblos • Kadesh

Damascus

CYPRUS

CRETE

LEBANON

Jerusalem

MEDITERRANEAN SEA

PALESTINE

CYRENACIA

LOWER EGYPT

SINAI

Fayyum

Memphis

ARABIA

Siwa Oasis

Bahariya Oasis

Akhet-aten (Amarna)

EASTERN DESERT

RED SEA

LIBYA

WESTERN DESERT

Farafra Oasis

Kharga Oasis

Thebes

Dakhla Oasis

UPPER EGYPT

Aswan

First Cataract

N

Second Cataract

Gebel Uweinat

River Nile

NUBIA

Fourth Cataract

Third Cataract

Fifth Cataract

Kerma

Napata

0   200 miles

Meroe

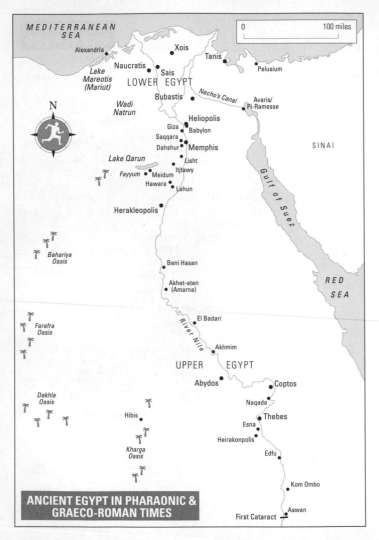

ANCIENT EGYPT IN PHARAONIC &
GRAECO-ROMAN TIMES

Egypt's Rise to Empire

THE HYKSOS: EGYPT UNDER
THE RULE OF FOREIGNERS

About **1650 BC**, following the period known as the Middle Kingdom, Egypt fell under the sway of a people called the **Hyksos** who established their capital at **Avaris** in the Nile Delta. In later times they were depicted by the Egyptians as foreign conquerors whose subjugation of the country and demands for tribute were a national humiliation. In fact the inhabitants of Avaris, whom the Egyptians called **Aamu**, their term for Near Eastern peoples (and whom Egyptologists refer to as Asiatics), were probably never an invading force but instead had settled peacefully in the Delta over time. Some were captives brought back from foreign campaigns, while others were traders and merchants who saw opportunities in developing commercial links between Egypt and the Levant. Indeed the archaeological evidence at Avaris suggests that the population was basically Egyptian but received influxes of immigrants from Palestine, Lebanon, Syria and Cyprus, whose prosperous elite married local women.

Who then were the Hyksos? The name derives from the Egyptian *hekau khasut* – 'rulers of foreign (literally mountainous) countries' – and was applied only to the rulers of the Asiatics. In other words a ruling caste from the hill country of the Near East imposed itself on the Aamu and others of Avaris. They did not come to Egypt as conquerors; rather, as centralized rule in Middle Kingdom Egypt collapsed, Avaris simply filled the vacuum of power. Indeed for the most part Hyksos rule was pacific; neither the Hyksos kings nor the Asiatics of Avaris and elsewhere in the Delta were much interested in Upper Egypt, from which they were content to receive tribute, and instead they preferred to look outwards to their ancestral lands in the Levant.

Hyksos contact with the **Near East** and the **Eastern Mediterranean** brought many innovations to Egypt, among them the vertical loom and an improved potter's wheel, new vegetable and fruit crops and also hump-backed cattle (*zebu*), new musical instruments and dances, the composite bow, the horse and chariot, and metallurgical expertise which allowed bronze to be manufactured locally, rather than having to rely on ready-alloyed imports. Thanks to the Hyksos, Egypt was put on a technological par with the wider world.

THEBES REVOLTS: ORIGINS OF THE 18TH DYNASTY

The Hyksos kingdom, based in Lower Egypt, included the entire **Delta** and also the lower **Nile Valley** as far south as present-day Beni Hasan. It also maintained communications and trade with its ally **Nubia**, far to the south via routes through the Western Desert oases. Nubia had long been under Egyptian control but had freed itself at the collapse of the Middle Kingdom.

Contemporaneous with the Hyksos 15th Dynasty at Avaris were the **16th and 17th Dynasty kings at Thebes** who ruled over Upper Egypt – that is everything between the Hyksos border at Beni Hasan to the north and the **Nubian frontier at Aswan** to the south. Thus, what had been under the central rule of an Egyptian pharaoh during the Middle Kingdom was now divided in three:

THE FORMIDABLE WOMEN OF THEBES

Brother-sister marriage in ancient Egypt preserved the divine royal blood from contamination, kept wealth and power in the family and cut down the number of potential pretenders to the throne. During the 18th Dynasty there was also an absolute prohibition – not there during the Old and Middle Kingdoms – against daughters of kings marrying anyone other than a reigning king. In the event, the sisters, wives and mothers of the 18th Dynasty proved to be women of formidable character and were remarkable for the various ways in which they advanced the fortunes of their line.

Amosis I, the first king of the 18th Dynasty, married **Ahmose-Nefertari**, who was probably the daughter of his mother Ahhotep, and his own full sister. He linked his family more closely to **Amun**, the local Theban deity who under the new dynasty would become a national god, by creating a new priesthood of Amun at Karnak and placing Ahmose-Nefertari in charge of it as God's Wife, an inheritable position which carried considerable religious and economic power. *continues over.*

The mortuary temple of Hatshepsut built against the cliffs of the Theban hills. Hatshepsut was a formidable woman who ruled Egypt with the title of king.

THE FORMIDABLE WOMEN OF THEBES (CONTD.)

Ahmose-Nefertari outlived her brother-husband and continued as God's Wife throughout the reign of their son **Amenophis I**. When he died without a male heir, it was most likely Ahmose-Nefertari who ensured the smooth succession of the non-royal **Tuthmosis I**, a warrior who laid the foundations for the Egyptian empire, by marrying him to Ahmose, who was probably her own daughter and a sister of Amenophis.

Tuthmosis II, the son of Tuthmosis I by a minor royal wife, married his half-sister Hatshepsut, who was the late king's daughter by his royal wife Amhose and also the God's Wife, a position she probably inherited from her grandmother Ahmose-Nefertari. But Hatshepsut failed to bear her husband a son, and before his premature death Tuthmosis II named his son by a concubine as his heir. This was **Tuthmosis III**, who eventually became a great warrior king and established the farthest limits of the empire. Yet during her lifetime, he was no match for **Hatshepsut,** whose character and proud claim to royal blood made her one of the most assertive of Theban women and one of Egypt's greatest rulers. In his youth she ruled in his place as regent, then, presenting herself in the regalia of a man, declared herself *king*, not queen, of Egypt. Entirely overshadowing Tuthmosis III, her nominal co-ruler, she devoted the remaining fifteen years of her life to Egypt's artistic revival, not least through her own mortuary temple at Deir el Bahri, one of the finest architectural achievements of all time.

A further chain of remarkable women was introduced into the 18th Dynasty when **Tuthmosis IV**, the grandson of Tuthmosis III, married a Mitannian princess as a secondary wife. The brother of this princess was **Yuya**, who became commander of the pharaoh's cavalry, and who married an Egyptian woman called **Tuyu**, by whom he had a daughter, **Tiy**, who, though she was a commoner, became the Great Royal Wife of Amenophis III, while her brother Ay became a general in the army.

The influence of Queen Tiy can be traced through the remarkable events of the next sixty years – to the death of Tutankhamun and its aftermath. One of her sons by Amenophis III became the so-called heretic pharaoh **Akhenaten** who completely revolutionised the religion and art of Egypt. His ally in promoting the worship of the sun disc Aten was his wife, the beautiful **Nefertiti**, who may well have been a niece of Tiy.

Tiy's granddaughter, **Princess Ankhesenamun**, who was the daughter of Nefertiti and Akhenaten, became the young bride of the boy-king Tutankhamun and his fiercely independent widow after his early death. Perhaps she was the person who placed the floral wreath upon her husband's head, the wreath that so touched Howard Carter when he came upon it three millenia later in Tutankhamun's burial chamber in the Valley of the Kings.

But also, as Carter knew, the royal blood ran in Ankhesenamun's veins and the divine breath filled her body, and as a king's daughter and a king's widow it lay uniquely within her power to confer kingship on any man she chose to marry, a circumstance which led to events of international intrigue and high drama (seee p.162).

Queen Tiy, the wife of Amenophis III and mother of Akhenaten. Her influence can be traced over the course of six decades to the death of Tutankhamun and beyond.

Hyksos, Theban and Nubian. But after nearly a century of this peaceful co-existence, Thebes launched the long struggle that once again would bring unity to the country.

The war against the Hyksos, begun by **Sekenenra** and carried forward by **Kamose**, kings of the 17th Dynasty ruling at Thebes, was brought to a successful end when **Amosis I** captured the Hyksos capital at Avaris. His swift follow-up campaign against Palestine and Syria and his southern campaign into Nubia laid the foundations for the **Egyptian empire**.

The rebirth of Egypt's fortunes under Amosis I explains why tradition marked his accession as the start of the **18th Dynasty**, though there was no break in the family line. Amosis' father was probably Sekenenra or possibly Kamose and his mother was **Ahhotep** – all three of whom were full or half-siblings. During the early years of Amosis' reign, while he was still in his minority, real power lay in the hands of his mother – the start of a tradition of strong women seen throughout the new dynasty.

EMPIRE, ARMY AND AMUN

The reunification of Egypt under the 18th Dynasty marked the beginning of a long period of stability, prosperity and empire known as the **New Kingdom**, which continued through the 19th and 20th Dynasties and lasted five hundred years.

The aim of **Egypt's imperial conquests**, which reached their greatest extent when the 18th Dynasty warrior kings **Tuthmosis I** and **Tuthmosis III** reached the Euphrates in Asia and the Fourth Cataract in Nubia, was to gain command over the routes of trade and the sources of raw materials – for agriculture, trade and Nubian gold were the basis of Egypt's wealth and power. By the close of **Amenophis III**'s reign, two centuries after the expulsion of the Hyksos, Egypt was wealthier and more powerful than it had ever been before. It was also at peace with its neighbours

Tuthmosis III is shown on the walls of the temple of Amun at Karnak in the characteristic pose of an 18th Dynasty warrior pharaoh: braining his enemies.

and no longer saw the world beyond its borders as hostile. Egypt became cosmopolitan in atmosphere, open to foreigners and their cultures, and its 18th Dynasty kings embellished their city of **Thebes** with great monuments and transformed it into the most opulent and important city in the ancient world.

But if the driving force in this success was the discipline and determination of the royal family, two other institutions became major beneficiaries of the imperial system – the army and the **priesthood of Amun**. The empire required a standing army, which if not on active service was kept employed in other ways, on major construction works for example, while army men and former officers increasingly filled many of the most important positions in the administration.

Amun, as the local god of Thebes, had grown in prominence with the rising fortunes of the town during the Middle Kingdom, and by the New Kingdom he was grafted onto Ra, the ancient sun god of Heliopolis, as **Amun-Ra**, king of the gods. Amun means hidden, and being an unseen god he took on the quality of being immanent everywhere, a suitably embracing and universal quality for a cosmopolitan and imperial age. The military conquests in Nubia and the Near East provided endowed lands for supporting Amun's priesthood and for building, enlarging and maintaining his temples in Egypt. Such was the triumvirate of the early 18th Dynasty – the priesthood, the army and the kingship, each one reinforced by the others.

Thebes: royal and holy city

18TH DYNASTY GLORY

Thebes was the name given by the Greeks to the city known to the ancient Egyptians as **Waset**. When Thebes was at the height of its glory during the 18th Dynasty, its population may have been as high as one million, and the city extended across both sides of the Nile. On the east bank (where modern **Luxor**, a town of 80,000 people, stands today) Thebes encompassed both the temple of Luxor to the south and the immense temple of Amun at Karnak two miles to the north, while it extended four miles along the west bank of the river, which it shared with the palace and pleasure lake of Amenophis III, the vast Theban necropolis which was the burial place of the elite, and several royal mortuary temples. The barren range of the Theban hills was on this western side too, and hidden within their rugged folds was the Valley of the Kings.

During the 18th Dynasty the wealth and talent of the world poured into Thebes, which was a cosmopolitan and universal city. Ships from Phoenicia and Nubia tied up at its quays to unload their precious cargoes from the Mediterranean and Africa or to deliver annual tributes of silver, gold, ebony, ivory, slaves and grain. Horses and the finest produce from the vineyards, orchards and pastures of Asia were imported, and exotic plants from Syria were grown in the botanical garden in the grounds of the temple of Amun. The Egyptians thought of Waset, filled with colour and spectacle, as the prototype of all cities and as the very spot where mankind first came into being.

> Waset is the pattern of every city,
> Both the flood and the earth were in her from the beginning of time,
> The sands came to delimit her soil,
> To create her ground upon the mound when the earth came into being.
> Then mankind came into being within her;
> To found every city in her true name
> Since all are called 'city' after the example of Waset.

The city remained proverbial for its wealth and power, and its fame was still remembered more than half a millennium later and on the far side of the Mediterranean when Homer composed these lines from *The Iliad*:

> Thebes of Egypt, where the houses are full of treasures, a city of a hundred gates, where through each of the gates two hundred men come forth to war with horses and chariots.

IMPERIAL DOMAINS AND TRADE

Victory over the Hyksos launched the kings of the 18th Dynasty on the path of empire. It immediately gave Egypt access to a network of cities and countries in the Near East that was highly developed both economically and culturally. **Southern Palestine**, the core region of the Hyksos, became Egyptian territory and served as a forward base for military expeditions deep into **Syria**, even as far as the Euphrates. Egypt sourced its timber, copper and oils and various other luxury goods from Palestine, Syria, **Mesopotamia** and **Persia**, and it traded as far as **Afghanistan**, which was the sole source for lapis lazuli. **Nubia** to the south of Egypt and formerly its colony was reconquered and became Egypt's most important area for raw materials. As a source of gold, Nubia was attractive to

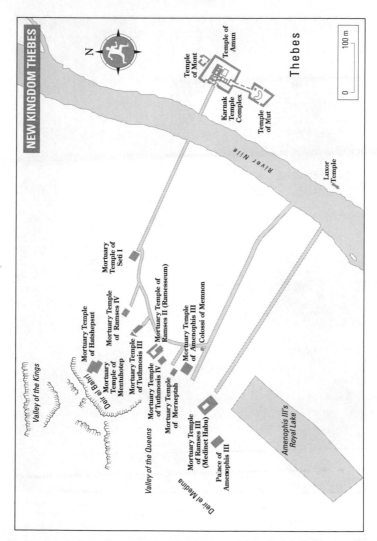

NEW KINGDOM THEBES

N

Thebes

Temple of Mont

Temple of Amun

Karnak Temple Complex

Temple of Mut

Luxor Temple

River Nile

Mortuary Temple of Seti 1

Mortuary Temple of Hatshepsut

Mortuary Temple of Ramses IV

Mortuary Temple of Mentuhotep

Mortuary Temple of Tuthmosis III

Mortuary Temple of Ramses II (Ramesseum)

Mortuary Temple of Amenophis III

Colossi of Memnon

Valley of the Kings

Deir el Bahri

Mortuary Temple of Tuthmosis IV

Mortuary Temple of Merneptah

Valley of the Queens

Mortuary Temple of Ramses III (Medinet Habu)

Palace of Amenophis III

Deir el Medina

Amenophis III's Royal Lake

0   100 m

Thebes rose to the zenith of its power and opulence during the long reign of Amenophis III. Egypt's empire extended from the Euphrates in the north to the fourth cataract of the Nile deep within Africa to the south.

the Egyptians; but it also provided skilled bowmen and other military recruits; minerals, wood, incense, cattle, slaves and hard building stone; and was an avenue of African trade.

Thebes' remoteness in the south of Egypt was an advantage as long as the Hyksos were in the north. But once the Hyksos were expelled and Upper and Lower Egypt had been reunited by the Theban warrior kings, the administration of the country was increasingly transferred north to **Memphis**, which – as in the Old Kingdom – became the administrative capital, a process that was effectively complete by the reign of Amenophis III. Nevertheless, the 18th Dynasty kings retained their **royal courts** at Thebes, which also remained their religious capital, so that they embellished the city with monuments, both to their posthumous selves in the form of mortuary temples, and above all to Amun, the victorious Theban god of national liberation. So powerful was Amun that the temple and priesthood of **Amun at Karnak** gradually came to form an alternative power base to that of the pharaohs (for more on which, see the following chapter).

As was common in ancient Egypt, the **houses, villas and palaces** of Thebes were built of mostly perishable materials, their roofs and screens of fronds and grasses, their walls of sun-dried mud brick – explaining why there is next to nothing of them to see today. Building in stone was reserved for the **temples** of the gods and **sanctuaries and tombs** of the king and the elite – and never before or later in Egyptian history was so much built in stone, nor were so many inscriptions, reliefs and murals worked on stone surfaces, as during the 250 years of the 18th Dynasty.

POWER AND PAGEANTRY: AMENOPHIS III AND TIY

The 18th Dynasty achieved its apogee during the reign of **Amenophis III** (c1390–c1352 BC). Not more than twelve when he came to the throne, Amenophis was still young when he married a commoner, **Tiy**, who bore the title of **Great Royal Wife** and became the most influential figure in his life. Amenophis also married a Babylonian and two Mitannian princesses, thus sealing Egypt's peaceful relations with the great powers of the Near East, and he vastly expanded trading relations with **Crete** and the **Greek mainland**.

Whether Egypt advanced as conqueror or as a trading power, the 18th Dynasty was marked by constant contacts with the peoples of Asia, Africa and the Mediterranean. The rapid increase of wealth that came from Egypt's exploitation of its empire in the Near East and Nubia was accompanied by a rapidly increasing taste for luxury, an **architecture of gigantic scale**, and a culture pervaded by an atmosphere of opulence. When people think of ancient Egypt, they are for the most part thinking of the New Kingdom, and especially the 18th Dynasty, for it was during this age of unparalleled confidence and prosperity that nearly every familiar great monument of Egyptian antiquity, the Pyramids excepted, was built – and the greatest builder in all Egyptian history was Amenophis III.

Amenophis built on both east and west sides of the Nile at Thebes in order to create an immense ceremonial stage for religious pageantry. He built most of the **temple of Luxor** which he dedicated to **Amun**, and he laid out the great processional way lined with sphinxes that connected it with Amun's great temple at **Karnak**, which he greatly magnified by building the third pylon and starting on the magnificent Hypostyle Hall. He also created a new royal area on the west bank of the Nile which included a palace and harem which he called the **House of Joy**, an enormous artificial lake and his own funerary temple guarded by gigantic statues of his divinised self, known to future generations as the **Colossi of Memnon**.

Once a year at the time of the famous **Festival of Opet**, Amun travelled on his golden barge with his wife Mut and their son the

The Colossi of Memnon are gigantic statues of Amenophis III that stood at the entrance to his now vanished mortuary temple across the Nile from Thebes.

moon god Khonsu in a floating procession of great splendour from Karnak to Luxor, where the god visited his harem of the south, returning to Karnak in refreshed glory some three weeks later. Once a year also, Amun crossed the Nile in his golden barge to celebrate the 'Beautiful Festival of the Valley' at the mortuary temple of Amenophis or some other, while the families of Thebes held overnight feasts in the tomb chapels, amid the music of harps, lutes, lyres and double pipes, the living and the dead united in one celebration.

THE SPECIAL ROLES OF TIY AND HER FATHER YUYA

Judging from how frequently and prominently **Queen Tiy** appeared alongside her husband in statues, reliefs and inscriptions, she was a woman of great influence; and, as such, she established a precedent for the prominence of Nefertiti in Akhenaten's reign. Though born a commoner, Tiy was nevertheless high-born. Her parents were **Yuya** and **Tuyu**, local aristocrats from the area around Akhmim, to the north of Thebes, who had close links to the royal court and the religious establishment, and who were – exceptionally – accorded burial in the Valley of the Kings. Tiy's son, who appointed her a close advisor, was the religious revolutionary Akhenaten; her brother may well have been Ay, who succeeded Tutankhamun as king; while Nefertiti, the beautiful wife of Akhenaten, may have been Ay's daughter and Tiy's niece.

Tiy therefore stands amid the swirl of what has been called 'the single most important event in Egypt's religious and cultural history': the **suppression of Amun** and the elevation of the **sun-disc Aten** to supreme deity by her son **Akhenaten**. It is not possible to say what role she or her family played, if any, in introducing the **new monotheistic religion**, but certainly she was its enthusiast through three generations. Tiy was there at the beginning, when she and her husband would sail across the pleasure lake he

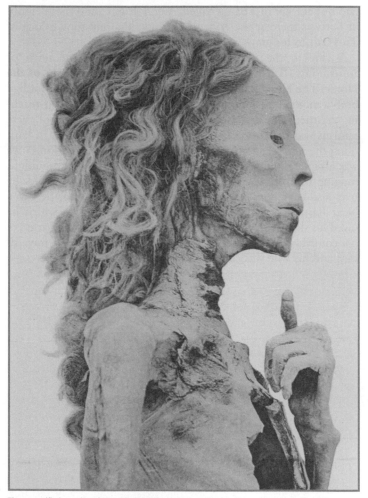

The mummified remains of 'the elderly lady' who is thought to be Queen Tiy. A lock of her hair was buried with her grandson Tutankhamun in his tomb.

had dug for her in a barge called 'Aten Gleams', and the memory of her was there at the end, when Tutankhamun took a lock of Tiy's hair to his grave.

A clue to the importance of Tiy's family in the reign of Amenophis III is found in her father Yuya's title, **Master of the Horse**. The Hyksos' introduction of the horse-drawn chariot had been a momentous military innovation, which led to a far-reaching restructuring of the Egyptian forces. At the centre of these reforms was the formation of an elite troop, specialised in handling the new weapons and in organising troop formation. Yuya was a representative of this new **military elite**, and intriguingly, judging from his name and from his features and his build, he may also have been a foreigner, with speculations that he was a Near Eastern or Mitannian prince, a background to which he owed his skills with the horse and chariot. Whatever the nature of his contribution was, the debt that Amenophis III felt towards him and his wife was considerable.

The Great God Amun

THE TEMPLE AT KARNAK

When Egypt stood at the height of empire, when Thebes ruled over Egypt, and when Amun was supreme over all, the **Temple of Amun at Karnak** possessed 81,000 slaves and their families, 240,000 head of cattle, 83 ships, and from 65 cities and towns their vast annual tribute in gold, silver, copper and precious stones.

Although the war god Mont, associated with Thebes during the Old Kingdom, continued to be worshipped at Karnak, **Amun** achieved pre-eminence by the beginning of the Middle Kingdom. With the expulsion of the Hyksos from Egypt and the elevation of Amun to victorious national god, the early pharaohs of the 18th Dynasty set about turning **Karnak** into the principal sanctuary of their kingdom. Amenophis I and his son Tuthmosis I built chapels around the Middle Kingdom temple, while in front of it the latter built the Fourth and Fifth Pylons and erected a pair of obelisks. Hatshepsut added two further obelisks between those of her father, chambers with carved decorations in front of the original temple, and initiated the north-south axis of the complex by building south. Her nephew Tuthmosis III continued building on this axis with the Seventh and Eighth Pylons, and constructed the Festival Hall behind the Middle Kingdom temple.

Amun in the temple at Karnak. As the power of Thebes extended over Egypt and its empire, so also grew the power of the priesthood of Amun, until it came into a fateful collision with the pharaoh Akhenaten.

DECLINE AND RENAISSANCE

In the century that passed between the Asian conquests of Tuthmosis III and the reign of Amenophis III, artistic and architectural restraint gave way to a grandiose imperial style, expressed at Karnak by the Third Pylon built by Amenophis III and his start on the great Hypostyle Hall. Empire introduced foreign influences and new wealth to the country, required an enlarged bureaucracy, and upset the status quo. Amun, who had lent his sword to the victories of the Theban kings, saw the coffers of his **priesthood** and of the **old aristocracy** from which it was drawn swell with tribute, and so their power grew.

However, another class, which owed its very existence to empire, was developing around the king. Tuthmosis IV married an Asian princess, and her son Amenophis III married Tiy, an Egyptian commoner. Tiy was given unusual artistic prominence alongside her husband, and her parents, Yuya and Tuyu, were buried in splendour in the Valley of the Kings. Pharaoh and temple no longer represented identical interests, and during the reign of **Amenophis IV** they were severed, as the pharaoh, who changed his name to **Akhenaten**, adopted the exclusive worship of Aten, and decamped to Amarna with his court (see the next chapter).

But the Amarna revolution did not survive the death of Akhenaten, and the reign of **Tutankhamun** marked the beginning of the counter-revolution which proceeded with a vengeance. The power of Amun was reaffirmed, and as though to sweep away all memory of heresy, internal conflict and the diminution of empire associated with the last pharaohs of the 18th Dynasty, **Seti I** of the 19th Dynasty declared his reign the era of the repeating of births, literally a renaissance. Both he and his son **Ramses II** outdid all that had gone before, both in architecture and in military propaganda, to make good any deficiencies in this assertion. Between them they completed the Hypostyle Hall.

The 19th Dynasty made its peace with Amun, but the cost in sacrificed wealth was greater than could be borne for long without the pharaoh becoming a mere creature of the priesthood. The Hypostyle Hall, the Ramesseum, Abu Simbel, may all have glorified Ramses II, but only through Amun who long survived that long-lived pharaoh. By the time **Ramses IV** of the 20th Dynasty came to the throne, 200 years after Akhenaten's reign and only 60 years after the death of Ramses II, the Temple of Amun owned at least seven percent of the population of Egypt and nine percent of the land, with some estimates trebling those percentages, while the family of the high priest of Amun directly controlled the collection of the king's taxes and management of the king's lands. The pharaoh had become no more than an instrument of a ruling oligarchy, and Karnak was its juggernaut.

Akhenaten: the heretic pharaoh

THE GROWING PROMINENCE OF THE SUN

During the reign of Amenophis III (1391–1553 BC) the worship of the sun – and the sun god **Ra** – grew ever more important to Egyptian religion. It became identified with almost every aspect of worship, so that the cults of many other of the gods, as well as that of the deified king himself, were increasingly solarised. At the very end of Amenophis' reign, hymns were composed that addressed the sun god as supreme, alone and distant in the sky, with all the other gods, as well as men and animals, part of his creation. Why this happened is not clear, but there is an argument that it was encouraged by Amenophis himself.

RA, AMUN AND ATEN

The 18th Dynasty pharaohs controlled immense material possessions, but the **priesthood of Amun** – which had linked their god to Ra – ran the royal house a close second. There is evidence that Amenophis III was conscious of the threat, and that he therefore promoted aspects of Ra independently of Amun. In particular, he enhanced the role of **Heliopolis**, which since earliest times had been the centre of the sun cult in Egypt, and had always enjoyed the closest religious and political ties with the kingship.

The temple at Heliopolis was the sanctuary of the sun god Ra, whose aspects were **Ra-Atum**, the creative force that brought the universe into being, and **Ra-Herakhte**, which was the sun itself. Publicly Amenophis promoted the worship of Ra-Herakhte, while at court he gave prominence to another solar diety, the **Aten** – the name by which the sun itself (and not the god immanent within it) had been known for many centuries. For example Amenophis gave the name 'Mansion of the Aten' to one of his estates, and he called queen Tiy's pleasure barge 'Aten Gleams'. In fact the two could be seen as one god, for though Aten could seem to have no meaning beyond 'sun', it could also be taken as a synonym for Ra-Herakhte.

But Amenophis III never lost sight of the various other gods of Egypt, even if he only saw them as aspects of the sun god. In particular he honoured **Osiris**, whom he saw as complementary to Ra, for death and the darkness of the underworld were positive and necessary states in the cycle of regeneration. For all that Amenophis tended towards a notion of divine unity, even as he attempted to restrict the power of the Amun-Ra priesthood, he took care to preserve the ages old tradition of plurality.

AMENOPHIS IV AT KARNAK

Whatever the intentions of Amenophis III, those of his son **Amenophis IV**, who would become the heretic king **Akhenaten**, were soon made clear. One of his first acts as pharaoh was to build a temple at the eastern end of the **Karnak** complex for Ra-Herakhte – a very large one, judging from the thousands of decorated blocks that have come to light. The god was represented in the same form as at Heliopolis, with the head of a falcon and a human body, but there was one important difference: his name was expanded to 'Ra-Herakhte of the horizon, who rejoices in the sunlight which is Aten'. This name was written in two parts, both

Amenophis IV, the future Akhenaten, is depicted on the wall of his new temple at Karnak making offerings to Aten, represented by the sun disc with hands at the ends of it emanating rays.

enclosed in cartouches like royal names, thereby implying that Amenophis IV regarded **Ra-Herakhte-Aten** as the king of the gods – precisely the epithet long borne by Amun-Ra.

Also at least one temple was built at Karnak for the new king's great royal wife, **Nefertiti**, who played an even more prominent role than Tiy had done during the previous reign. Nefertiti was depicted assisting the king in all his cultic activities, and was herself shown in postures normally reserved to the king alone, such as triumphally smiting enemies, which symbolised subduing the powers of chaos, and **presenting Maat**, which meant maintaining the balance and harmony of the universe. When Nefertiti and Amenophis IV performed rituals together, they enacted the roles of **Shu**, the god of air and sunlight, and his twin sister-wife **Tefnut**, the first pair of divinities to issue from the androgynous creator god **Atum** (a bust of Akhenaten in the current exhibition shows him wearing the four-feathered headdress of Shu). What has become known as the **Amarna style** of Egyptian art first

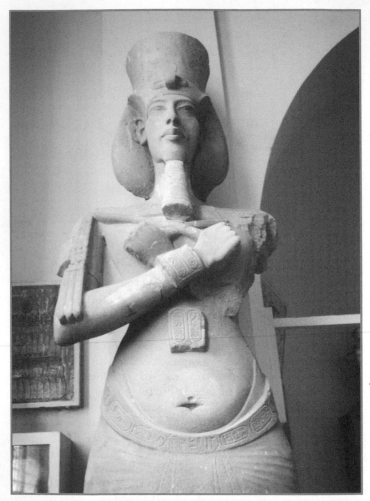

A colossal statue of Amenophis IV from Karnak shows him with a long narrow face and pendulous belly in what became the full-blown Amarna style.

appeared at these shrines at Karnak – statues and reliefs with elongated features, and in the case of the king the pendulous belly, swollen thighs and almost feminine breasts which were meant to suggest the male and female aspects of the creator god.

Soon Amenophis IV weakened the link with Heliopolis. The god was no longer represented in the guise of falcon-headed Ra-Herakhte, but as the **sun's disc** whose rays reached out to the king and his wife Nefertiti and their children, offering them the **ankh**, the sign of life but also of dominion or power. Significantly no priesthood intervened; the king alone was shown as the intercessor between mankind and the Aten.

Not that he was even now determined to break with the **Amun priesthood**. Indeed there are reliefs made during these first four years of his reign showing him worshipping Amun. Yet the evidence is contradictory, for it was also at this time that the high priest of Amun was sent to a desert quarry. Perhaps the resistance he met from the priesthood goaded Amenophis to go further, and perhaps too he received encouragement from Nefertiti (who may well have been the daughter of Ay and the granddaughter of Yuya and Tuyu), who played an enigmatic but central role throughout the Amarna drama. Amenophis IV had already begun diverting revenues from the priesthood of Amun to the cult of Aten. But now his programme went far beyond bringing the priesthood to heel, and he seems to have been driven by a genuine and impassioned **vision of the divine**. In any case, he soon recognised that no compromise was possible, and that he needed to remake the world, starting with his own sacred city, where there would be no other gods but Aten.

Akhenaten at Amarna

In the fourth year of his reign, Amenophis IV, accompanied by Nefertiti, visited the site of his intended new religious capital,

Akhet-aten – 'The Horizon of the Aten' – which stood on the east bank of the Nile 200 miles north of Thebes at a place now called **Amarna** or Tell el Amarna. No settlement had stood there before, nor was the place associated with any gods. During their visit he issued a proclamation which set out the plan of his city, the axes of its avenues, the location of its quarters, and where its palaces and temples should be.

Looking towards the great crescent wall of cliffs which enclosed the site on the east, with rocky valleys running back up to the desert plateau beyond, he also ordered that **tombs** should be constructed there for his family and himself, a break with the tradition of his dynasty, which for 150 years had been buried in the Valley of the Kings. 'My tomb will be hollowed in the Eastern Mountain, my burial will be made there in the multitude of jubilees which Aten my Father has ordained for me,' Akhenaten

Akhenaten built his new capital, Akhet-aten, at a beautiful virgin site between the Nile and a sweeping crescent of cliffs where no god had ruled before. Today it is occupied by a simple village called Amarna.

Akhenaten's wife Nefertiti is depicted here on a fragment from her sanctuary at Karnak in extreme early Amarna style. Fashionably avant-garde, she wears a wig which imitates the Nubian military hair-style.

proclaimed, 'and the burial of the great royal wife Nefertiti will take place there in the multitude of years.'

Amenophis IV then changed his name (which means 'Amun is Content') to **Akhenaten** ('Creative Manifestation of Aten'); while Nefertiti, whose name means 'the Beautiful One has Come', added the name **Neferneferuaten**, 'Beautiful is the Beauty of Aten'. And in about the sixth year of his reign, Akhenaten took up residence at Akhet-aten and issued a proclamation vowing that the city would always belong to Aten: 'Akhet-aten belongs to Aten my father like the mountains, deserts, the fields, the islands, the upper lands and the lower lands, the water, the villages, the men, the animals and all those things to which Aten my father will give life eternally. I shall not neglect the oath which I have made to Aten my father for eternity.' As his foreign office files, the famous **Amarna Letters**, have been excavated here, it seems likely that Akhet-aten served also as the seat of government.

Here at Akhet-aten in temples open to the sun, Aten was worshipped to the exclusion of all other gods. Akhenaten himself composed the new **Hymn to the Sun** in which he discarded myth, convention and abstraction, and spoke of the sensate reality of Aten which creates, embraces and expresses all existence:

At dawn you rise shining in the horizon, you shine as Aten in the sky and drive away darkness by sending forth your rays. The Two Lands awake in festivity, and men stand on their feet, for you have raised them up. They wash their bodies, they take their garments, and their arms are raised to praise your rising. The whole world does its work.

The cattle are content in their pasture, the trees and plants are green, the birds fly from their nests. Their wings are raised in praise of your soul. The goats leap on their feet. All flying and fluttering things live when you shine for them. Likewise the boats race up and down the river, and every way is open, because you have appeared. The fish in the river leap before your face. Your rays go to the depths of the sea.

You set the germ in women and make seed in men. You maintain the son in the womb of the mother and soothe him so that he does not weep, you nurse in the womb. You give the breath of life to all you have created. When the child comes forth from the womb on the day of his birth, you open his mouth and you supply his needs. The chick in the egg can be heard in the shell, for you give him breath inside it so that he may live. You have given him in the egg the power to break it. He comes out of the egg to chirp as loudly as he can; and when he comes out, he walks on his feet.

From the ninth year of his reign, Akhenaten required that Aten be worshipped not merely as the supreme god but as the **only god**. Moreover, Akhenaten himself was the god's high priest through whom all the prayers of the people must be transmitted. In the same year he dropped the name Herakhte, so that Aten was only ever combined with **Ra** – the one survival from the entire Egyptian pantheon, because Ra was the god in whom the true god, the Aten, had always existed. Akhenaten then set about **closing the temples** of all gods other than Aten throughout the land.

Monotheism was first introduced to history by Akhenaten. He banned the traditional religion of Egypt with its multiple gods and insisted on the worship of one god only.

The name Amun was everywhere hacked out, and sometimes also the word 'gods' in plural – a vast undertaking which required the army's help.

Akhenaten was no pacifist. The Amarna Letters (the diplomatic archives found at Akhet-aten) show that Egypt was involved in continuous **military activity** in northern Syria, mostly to prevent its local vassals from changing sides and giving their support to the rising Hittite empire. And Akhenaten sent the army into Nubia to quash a rebellion there in his twelfth regnal year. Likewise the role of the army in his religious revolution was probably vital. The military presence is evident on the reliefs from his shrines at Karnak and in the rock-cut tombs at Akhet-aten, where a bodyguard of predominantly blacks and Asians surround the king to prevent any resistance. Akhenaten has been called the first to found a new religion. Certainly he is the only historical figure known to have founded a religion with the benefit of all the instruments of state power at his disposal.

As the creative manifestation of the Aten, the king 'made' his people, especially the elite, who now denied their family backgrounds, however eminent, and said they owed everything to the king. Piety towards the Aten was identical with absolute loyalty to Akhenaten, through whom they were ensured **life after death**, for Osiris too had been proscribed and no longer sat in judgement on their souls. From being a representative theocracy in which Amun had acted through the king, Egypt became a direct **theocracy** with the king as the manifestation of Aten acting directly in everyday life and the afterlife.

AKHENATEN'S WOMEN

Akhenaten's mother was **Tiy**, the widow of Amenophis III. She is known to have made a state visit to Akhet-aten in her son's twelfth regnal year, and probably she spent time there, where she

Akhenaten, left, and Nefertiti appear with their daughters beneath the rays of the sun disc Aten, whom Egyptians were expected to worship through the royal family.

would have had her own palace and temple. Akhenaten appointed her as one of his advisors, alongside Nefertiti and her father Ay, and it is evident from the Amarna Letters that she enjoyed prestige abroad for shrewdness and wisdom. Tiy's brother had been a high priest of the sun god at Heliopolis, but his views and what influence he might have had on Akhenaten are unknown. For that matter Tiy's own views on her son's religious venture are not known, only that her funerary rites were carried out in accordance with the new dispensation, and that she was buried in a rock tomb in the cliffs overlooking Akhet-aten.

Nefertiti, who was Akhenaten's great royal wife, was frequently depicted with the king in a display of harmonious union and in her role as **fertile consort**. A relief from one of Akhenaten's sanctuaries at Karnak even shows her about to get into bed with her husband. Nefertiti bore Akhenaten at least six daughters, the three eldest within the first six or seven years of his reign. The first born was **Meritaten**, who would later, after the apparent disappearance of Nefertiti, become wife and queen to her father, possibly bearing him a daughter. Subsequently she became wife and queen to the mysterious and short-reigning **Smenkhkere**. The second daughter, **Meketaten**, died in about the twelfth year of her father's reign; her parents, joyful children of the solar disc, were painted on the walls of her sarcophagus chamber in sad mourning. The third daughter, **Ankhesenpaaten**, became the wife and queen of Tutankhamun.

Nefertiti may also have borne Akhenaten sons, but whereas the daughters are often shown with their parents, no son is ever depicted. But this does not mean that there were no sons; rather, it would not have been in line with 18th Dynasty artistic decorum for sons, who were reminders of their father's mortality and raised questions about the succession, to have the same presence as daughters, in whom continuity resided. Also, with increasing **solarisation** – which was already being felt long before Akehanaten, possibly during the reign of Tuthmosis IV, and most certainly during that of his son Amenophis III – royal ideology required the king to present himself as a **manifestation of the sun god**. This solarised persona of the king was complemented by the appearance of women – Tiy in the case of Amenophis III, Nefertiti in the case of Akhenaten – as well as other female relations, for whom mythology provided roles. Sons had no such roles.

With the suppression of the traditional pantheon, **Nefertiti** inevitably became more important as a manifestation of the divine. At the beginning of Akhenaten's reign, Nefertiti played Tefnut to his Shu, completing the triad at whose head stood the creator god Atum. Now Nefertiti again played a part in a **divine triad**, this time as a divine emanation of Aten whose beneficent

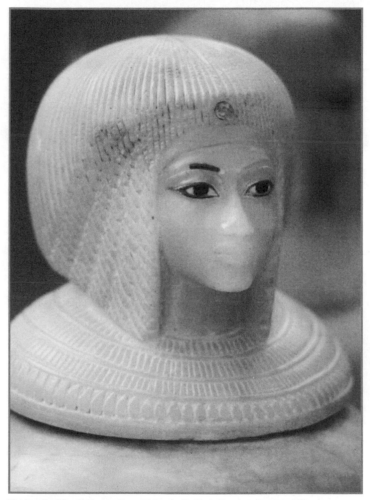

Kiya bore the title of Akhenaten's great beloved wife. She is thought to have born Akhenaten a son who eventually came to the throne as Tutankhamun.

Nefertiti represented in late Amarna style, when it had softened, and her beauty is rendered in exquisitely elegant form.

rays extended towards both Akhenaten and herself. In Akenaten's tomb at Akhet-aten, Nefertiti stood at all four corners of his sarcophagus, in the positions occupied by Isis, Nephthys, Neith and Selkis on the sarcophagus of Tutankhamun, so that it was Nefertiti who in the absence of the traditional funerary deities became Akhenaten's protective goddess.

Apart from Nefertiti, Akhenaten had other wives, and probably had children by them. One of these wives who achieved prominence for a while was **Kiya**, whose name appeared on official monuments at Akhet-aten. While Nefertiti remained the king's great royal wife, Kiya was distinguished with the singular title of great beloved wife, though she never fulfilled a religious role nor ever wore a crown. She was sometimes represented with a daughter, a child of the king, but her chief historical interest is the likelihood that she bore Akhenaten a son, the child described in an inscription as 'the king's bodily son, his beloved, **Tutankhaten**', the name that **Tutankhamun** had been given at birth.

AMARNA ART

After briefly being portrayed in the traditional way at the beginning of his reign, Amenophis IV had himself depicted with a **thin drawn face** which was interrupted by thick lips before arriving at a pointed chin. The rest of his body was no less distorted, indeed it was at this early period that the distortion was the greatest, his **neck** elongated, his **breasts** full and almost like those of a woman, his hips wide, his thighs fat and his legs thin and spindly. Not only Akhenaten was depicted in this way but also Nefertiti and their daughters, and to a lesser degree of exaggeration all other human beings as well.

The point in Akhenaten's case of this form of representation was explained by his own pronouncement, that he was **'the mother who gives birth to everything'**. In other words, like the androgynous creator god, who was said to have made mankind in his own image, Akhenaten presented himself in terms of male and female elements. Later in his reign a more balanced style developed, and busts of Nefertiti portray nothing less than an exquisitely elegant and beautiful woman.

Some see nothing more in Akhenaten's peculiar representations of himself than religious ideology. Others think the **reliefs and statues** must be to some degree based on reality and have gone so far as to diagnose the king as suffering from the most physically distorting diseases. There is controversy over whether his mummy has been found; it may have been that inside the coffin found in Tomb 55 in the Valley of the Kings. If so, then no great distortion of physical form has been noted.

The **distortions in Amarna art** can be seen as an assault on the then prevailing conception of the world as static, where everything was fixed in its place for eternity. Egyptian art worked its scenes and persons by using an **underlying grid**; everything is rigorously presented in terms of verticals and horizontals – to which Amarna art opposes slashing **diagonals** and the beat and rhythm of bold **contours**. Complementing this is an extraordinary sense of **movement and speed**. You see it in treatments of nature, for example the fluttering of birds wings on the murals which decorated the royal palace at Akhet-aten, while an ecstasy of speed pervades the **chariot scenes**, which depict not just the usual hunts and battles but the rapid transport of the king; Akhenaten seems to have taken to chariots in the same way that princes of a later age would take to fast open-topped cars, he and Nefertiti speeding along clutched in an embrace, streamers billowing from their crowns. And with motion came emotion, so that Amarna art is pervaded by a playfulness and a freedom of expression, and an intimacy between the king and queen, depicting kisses and caresses, that had never before been seen in Egyptian art.

Amarna art could be vividly naturalistic as in this fragment of paving from Akhenaten's south palace at Akhet-aten.

AMARNA BELIEFS AND THE AFTERLIFE

Akhenaten received his revelation directly from the Aten, but he left no holy book. Instead what we have is Akhenaten's **Hymn to the Sun**, and it is to that which we must look for an outline of his beliefs. The Hymn dispenses with mythic images and primeval creation, which it replaces with the contemplation of nature. Aten is universal; the sun shines on all mankind.

Atenism was the first attempt to explain the entire natural and human world in terms of a single principle, which was **light**. Ultimately Aten was not the sun disc, rather the light which is in the sun and radiates from it, the generator of life. Free from all mythic associations, it is a very pure and focused conception, which has been called the world's **first monotheistic religion**. And leaving aside Aten's triad with the royal couple, Akhenaten's monotheism is certainly more rigorous than that of the Old Testament, or of the Koran.

Traditional Egyptian temples were narrower, lower, darker as the worshipper advanced towards the sanctuary where its cult image was locked away from the light – not that anyone did advance so far, except the king and priests. But Atenism's god was there for all to see; no images were necessary, only the open sky. And so the **temples of Aten** were great open-air courts where the favourite offering was flowers. In fact at Akhet-aten the entire city was conceived as a sacred microcosm; wherever you went, you walked on holy ground.

The orientation of Akhet-aten was to the **east**, to the **rising sun** which was the source of life. The west and the underworld did not figure, nor did the judgement of Osiris: his worship was sup-

Akhet-aten was razed to the ground by Ramses II and never built on again. The remains of the palaces and temples once frequented by Akhenaten and Nefertiti can just be discerned amid the palms and the drifting sand.

pressed even before Amun's. Unlike at Thebes, the tomb decorations at Akhet-aten did not concern themselves with the afterlife; instead they were decorated with vivid scenes of the everyday. Ay, for example, who was Akhenaten's master of horse and possibly Nefertiti's father, and who would succeed Tutankhamun as pharaoh, originally had a tomb prepared for himself at Akhet-aten which was never used and is the best preserved today. In one scene, Ay and his wife are shown receiving golden collars from Akhenaten and Nefertiti while guards and onlookers outside the palace react to the honour and excitement of it all. There are street scenes, closely observed and marvellously true to life, and peeps of palace intimacy, with a lady of the harem having her hair done, some girls playing the harp and dancing, while others prepare the food and sweep the floor. Also, on one side of the doorway of Ay's tomb is the most complete and probably the most correct version of Akhenaten's Hymn to the Sun.

In a sense there was no longer an **afterlife**, and certainly there was no underworld; the dead in the form of their **ba** were to live in the daylight of now. All was now, all was light, and though ideally the *ba* united with the body for completion, the mummy was no longer necessary. It follows that there was no Book of the Dead in the Amarna period. The temple and the palace were the new realm of the dead; the *ba* visited the nearest one, rather than accompanying the sun in his solar boat. Such afterlife as there was amounted to nothing more than a good night's sleep. The dead slept at night, and in daytime they accompanied the Aten to one of the temples to be provisioned.

Numerous altars were set up in the open courts of the temples where the dead were provisioned by the king. Akhenaten took over the role of Osiris in that he controlled provisions for the afterlife; the skies may have been open, the sun there for all to see, but all prayers to the Aten and all provisions from the Aten had to pass through the king.

EGYPT BEYOND AMARNA

Much of what is known about Akhenaten's life is derived from reliefs on the walls of his **courtiers' tombs** cut into the rock at Akhet-aten. They show the royal family, their private and public activities, and above all their devotion to the worship of Aten; but the scenes are restricted to events at Akhet-aten, and nothing is revealed about what the king was doing, or neglecting to do, in the country at large.

It is known that Akhenaten built temples to Aten round Egypt, including one at Memphis and another at Heliopolis, and also at least one in Nubia. And it is known that in suppressing the worship of the old gods and closing their temples, he directed his energies heavily at Thebes. Yet judging even from what was going on inside Akhet-aten, where images of gods from the traditional pantheon have been found within the remains of the houses of common people, the vast majority of Egyptians probably continued in their **pre-Amarna beliefs**. Akhenaten's policy, in which he probably succeeded, was to target the elite, the people who owed their positions to his authority, especially in Akhet-aten itself, and to strike against resistance in Thebes. Much depended on his energy, his character and his personal conviction; in the event his religious revolution barely survived his passing.

THE COLLAPSE

Nefertiti's name vanishes from the records after about the fourteenth year of Akhenaten's reign. Possibly she died, though there is no evidence of it; or possibly she and her husband fell out over policy; or perhaps she was put aside for Kiya who bore the title of the Great Beloved Wife and who appears on the scene at about this time. In any case, from the fourteenth regnal year until Akhenaten's death in about his seventeenth regnal year Nefertiti's

The bust of an Amarna princess, probably Meritaten, who seems to have become consort to her father after the 'disappearance' of Nefertiti – but then later Meritaten may have married her own mother.

place as consort to the king was taken by her daughter **Meritaten**, who according to the inscriptions then married **Smenkhkere**, a figure of unknown origin.

Nothing indicates that Akhenaten was violently overthrown. But at his death he had no disciples to carry on his work; he had concentrated everything on himself, and the circle of his followers were bereft of a reference point. Soon the sole worship of the Aten was abandoned, along with the ban on the pantheon of gods and the denial of an afterlife in the underworld, and gradually Egyptians returned to their old beliefs.

Smenkhkere seems to have ruled as co-regent for three years but did not survive Akhenaten's death by longer than a few months; during what little time he had, there is evidence of a **rapprochement with the Theban priesthood**, and possibly he spent the latter part of his co-regency in residence at Thebes.

But immediately there is a mystery. On one view, Smenkhkere adopted the name 'Beautiful is the Beauty of Aten', formerly Nefertiti's name, as an indication that he continued to adhere to Atenism. But as it happens his co-regency lasted for exactly as long as Nefertiti went 'missing', and it may be that it was not Smenkhkere who adopted Nefertiti's name but **Nefertiti** who adopted the name Smenkhkere and spent those 'missing' three years co-ruling with Akhenaten. Perhaps Akhenaten had become severely ill, and it had been necessary for Nefertiti to adopt a male persona to share in the kingship, not unlike Hatshepsut before her. Then at Akhenaten's death Nefertiti in the male persona of Smenkhkere would have married Meritaten, her own daughter.

At any rate, after the passing of Smenkhkere, whoever he or she was, the crown passed to **Tutankhamun**, or rather **Tutankhaten** as he was then known – the only remaining royal male member of the 18th Dynasty.

AKHENATEN SUPERSTAR

No pharaoh has excited such passionate interest as **Akhenaten,** whose break with Egyptian tradition has cast him as the precursor of modern man. He has been compared to Moses, Jesus Christ, Julian the Apostate, St Francis of Assisi, Leonardo da Vinci, Martin Luther and Oliver Cromwell, and his reign evokes associations with the Protestant Reformation, the English Civil War, the French Revolution, the Russian Revolution ... in fact, almost any conflict involving ideology and religion. The pharaoh has even been co-opted into sexual politics, adopted as the first homosexual, transvestite and hermaphrodite. And he has inspired theologies, novels, operas, paintings and films.

In some respects, the Akhenaten story, which emerged in the late nineteenth century, prepared the ground for the world's excitement at the discovery of Tutankhamun's tomb. But even then, Akhenaten remained for many the compelling figure: Tutankhamun representing the embalmed image of Egypt as a land obsessed with death, while Akhenaten and the Amarna period offered something more thrilling – an archaeology of life. All the same, the public fascination with each figure reinforced its interest in the other, for both Akhenaten and Tutankhamun are part of that remarkable story which is the **Amarna period and the 18th Dynasty**.

BIRTH OF A CULTURE HERO
The first firm identification of **Akhenaten** at **Akhet-aten** with **Amenophis IV**, son of Amenophis III at Thebes, was made by Karl Richard Lepsius, a Prussian, who visited the **Amarna** site in 1843 and 1845. Lepsius also found evidence that Akhenaten had opposed the worship of Amun with a 'pure cult of the sun' and had hacked away the images of the old gods. The first systematic investigation of Akhenaten's capital was carried out by Sir Flinders Petrie with the assistance of Howard Carter in 1891–92, and in 1895 James Henry Breasted translated Akhenaten's **Hymn to the Sun**.

'To his own nation', wrote Breasted in his 1905 *History of Egypt*, 'Akhenaten was afterward known as the criminal of Akhet-aten; but for us ... there died with him such a spirit as the world had never seen before – a brave soul, undauntedly facing the momentum of immemorial

continues over.

tradition, and thereby stepping out from the long line of conventional and colourless Pharaohs, that he might disseminate ideas far beyond and above the capacity of his age to understand. Among the Hebrews, seven or eight hundred years later, we look for such men; but the modern world has yet adequately to value or even acquaint itself with this man, who in an age so remote and under conditions so adverse, became the world's first idealist and the world's first individual.'

Breasted's *History* was the first account of ancient Egypt based on all available archaeological sources. Now it was possible to read in one grand sweep the story of Egypt's pharaonic past, and though Akhenaten had until then hardly been overlooked, he was confirmed by America's founding father of Egyptology as a prophet before his time. In 1910 the first biography of the pharaoh appeared: Arthur Weigall's breathless *The Life and Times of Akhnaton, Pharaoh of Egypt*, an emotive mix of archaeology, religion and romance that became a bestseller. Atenism, Weigall wrote, was a 'religion so pure that we must compare it to Christianity in order to discover its faults'. He compared the sun disc with its rays to the Christian cross, and Akhenaten's *Hymn to the Sun* to the teachings of St Francis of Assisi and to Psalm 104:

He appointed the moon for seasons: the sun knoweth his going down.
Thou makest darkness, and it is night: wherein all the beasts of the forest do
*   creep forth.*
The young lions roar after their prey, and seek their meat from God.
The sun ariseth, they gather themselves together, and lay them down in
*   their dens.*
Man goeth forth unto his work and to his labour until the evening.

Taken together, Breasted's history and Weigall's biography had an enormous impact on the public, and the books laid the foundations for one of the most persistent ideas about Akhenaten, that he was a benign proto-Christ figure, and that his message of monotheism had somehow survived and been passed on.

MOSES AND MONOTHEISM

It is from **Manetho**, an Egyptian priest and historian of the third century BC, that we have a list of kings and dynasties with their years that serves as the basis for all chronologies of Ancient Egypt. He lived at a time, following the conquest of Egypt by Alexander the Great, when the Ptolemies, a Greek dynasty, ruled Egypt. Manetho seems to have had some knowledge of Akhenaten's reign, perhaps from temple archives or oral histories, and he tells several stories that could preserve recollections from the past. There is an anecdote of Amenophis III being warned by a seer that Egypt would suffer thirteen years of disaster, and another recalling a mass migration of 80,000 people to a remote place on the east bank of the Nile which later is abandoned. Are these vague memories of the unsettled times during Akhenaten's heresy, and the settlement of Akhet-aten? Manetho also mentions successors to Amenophis III who bear names like Akencheres or Akencherses, which could be Akhenaten.

In later centuries, other versions of ancient Egyptian history were in circulation, possibly derived from Manetho, which share a strong tradition of connecting Moses with a period of upheaval in Egypt lasting thirteen years, a period marked by religious iconoclasm and political brutality. One of these, written by the first century AD Jewish historian **Josephus**, links **Moses** to a folkloric version of Akhenaten. However, there are several problems about linking Moses to Akhenaten. One is chronology. Akhenaten died in about **1338 BC**, but the **Exodus** is usually associated with Ramses II's son **Merneptah** who ruled from about **1213 to 1205 BC**. Further, that begs the question of whether there was an Exodus at all. The Egyptian records make no mention of it, while the biblical account was written sometime between the ninth and fifth centuries BC and is otherwise unsupported by any historical evidence whatsoever. Indeed, many scholars believe that there was no Exodus from Egypt, and that it was a founding myth of the Israelites, added at a later stage.

But a good story is a good story, especially if it is told in the Bible, touched on by Josephus, and helped along if not entirely intentionally by Egyptologists. **Sigmund Freud** was very excited by Breasted's and Weigall's books, especially by Weigall's account of Akhenaten's childhood, which has him raised by an overbearing mother in Tiy and a passive father in Amenophis III. Of course Weigall could not

continues over.

AKHENATEN SUPERSTAR *CONTD.*

have had the slightest idea about the nature of Akhenaten's parents or anything else about his childhood, and he only called his book 'a sketch'. But Freud leapt at Weigall's account as objective proof taken from antiquity for the existence of the Oedipus Complex, which in this case explained why Akhenaten overthrew Amun and set up a new god in the Aten – because he had a jealous sexual hatred for his father and sexual desire for his mother.

Having gone that far, Freud went further, and in his book *Moses and Monotheism* announced that Moses was an Egyptian, not a Jew. 'Let us assume that Moses was a noble and distinguished man, perhaps indeed a member of the royal house, as the myth has it. He must have been conscious of his great abilities, ambitious, and energetic; perhaps he saw himself in a dim future as the leader of his people, the governor of the Empire. In close contact with Pharaoh, he was a convinced adherent of the new religion, whose basic principles he fully understood and had made his own. With the king's death and the subsequent reaction he saw all his hopes and prospects destroyed. If he was not to recant the convictions so dear to him, then Egypt had no more to give him; he had lost his native country. In this hour of need he found an unusual solution. The dreamer Akhenaten had estranged himself from his people, had let his world empire crumble. Moses' active nature conceived the plan of founding a new empire, of finding a new people, to whom he could give the religion that Egypt disdained. It was, as we perceive, a heroic attempt to struggle against his fate, and to find compensation in two directions for the losses he had suffered through Akhenaten's catastrophe. Perhaps he was at the time governor of that border province (Goshen) in which – perhaps already in the Hyksos period – certain Semitic tribes had settled. These he chose to be his new people. A historic decision!'

Once you have gone that far with Breasted, Weigall and Freud, you might as well go the whole hog with contemporary Egyptian writer **Ahmed Osman** who has made something of a career writing bestselling books assigning biblical identities to historical Egyptians. For example, in his *Out of Egypt*, published in 1998, Osman argues that Yuya was really Joseph, Tuthmosis III really

David and Amenophis III in fact Solomon. Also Tiy was the mother of Moses, which makes Moses and Akhenaten one and the same people, while Nefertiti was Moses' sister Miriam. And then, never mind a missing thousand years or so, Tutankhamun was really Jesus. Osman's book – a kind of Old Testament *Da Vinci Code* – is currently being adapted as a major motion picture.

TYRANNY IN THE NAME OF TRUTH

A much more thoughtful and worthwhile book has been written by the Egyptian Nobel Prize winning novelist **Naguib Mahfouz**. Published in 1985, *Akhenaten: Dweller in the Truth* depicts a king who has a mystical revelation and discovers a god, one god, the sole creator, who is the god of love, forgiveness and peace. But when Akhenaten prohibits the worship of any god other than his One God, he shows himself to be fanatic determined to impose his idea of truth on a diverse and sophisticated people. Whether he is right or not becomes less important than the chaos which ensues. The book was written as Islamic fundamentalism was becoming all the more pervasive and intimidating in Egypt. Indeed in 1994 Mahfouz almost lost his life when he was stabbed by an Islamist after condemning the fatwa issued by Ayatollah Khomeini, leader of the Iranian revolution, against Salman Rushdie for writing *The Satanic Verses*.

The Egyptologist **Nicholas Reeves**, an expert on Tutankhamun and the Amarna period, sees Akhenaten more in line with Mahfouz, and believes that Egypt under the enforced faith of Aten was cruel and dictatorial. 'Akhenaten was closer to Stalin, Hitler, and Mao than the proto-Christ portrayed by Arthur Weigall,' he suggests.

What does at least seem certain is that Akhenaten is interpreted anew by each generation. But whether this is to suit its own experience of the world, or because it has come to a closer understanding of the world of Akhenaten, remains open to question.

The Akhenaten story as fundamentalist allegory.

The life of Tutankhamun

WHO EXACTLY WAS THE BOY-KING?

One disappointment attended Howard Carter's discovery of Tutankhamun's tomb. For all its gold and treasure and insights into the past, it provided no significant **inscriptions** or other documentary evidence about the life and times of the young man who lay sheathed within his coffins inside the burial chamber. Therefore the biographical and historical picture has to be assembled from other sources – and frankly the gaps are large and the room for interpretation is considerable.

At the most basic level, Tutankhamun's **parentage** is uncertain; it is unknown even if he was of **royal stock**. The documentation on Tutankhamun was so slight that Carter speculated on the possibility that he may well have been born a mere commoner, though since then, an inscription has been found across the Nile from Amarna which describes Tutankhamun as the son of a king. It has been suggested that he was a late son of **Amenophis III**, but as Tutankhamun died around 1327 at about the age of 19 and Amenophis IV came to the throne in about 1352, that assumption works only if one assumes that the accession of the younger Amenophis did not mark the death of his father, and that the elder Amenophis was co-ruler of Egypt with his son for several years. The body of opinion among Egyptologists, however, is that a co-regency, if there was one at all, was very short. In which case the royal father in the inscription which refers to 'the king's bodily son, his beloved, Tutankhaten' must have been **Akhenaten**.

Who then was the mother of Tutankhamun? **Nefertiti** is generally ruled out because, though she had at least six daughters, she is not known to have had a son. But, as explained on p.136, there were reasons why there would be little or no official recognition of sons as opposed to daughters. Nevertheless most Egyptologists look to a secondary wife of Akhenaten, and mostly they single out a lovely young woman in his harem called **Kiya**, who was possibly a Mitannian princess. The king bestowed on Kiya the unique title of Great Beloved Wife, and perhaps that tells it all, though she too was depicted only with a daughter, never with a son. Kiya disappears from the records at about the time that Tutankhamun was born, leading to speculation that she died in childbirth, though plague was also current and probably accounted for the death of Akhenaten's and Nefertiti's daughter Meketaten in about that same year.

Yet ultimately the royal status of Tutankhamun did not depend upon his parents, for according to Egyptian ideology the kingship was transmitted through the female line, and so his right to the throne was established by his marriage to **Ankhesenpaaten**, the third daughter of Akhenaten and Nefertiti, who was most likely his sister or half-sister. Tutankhamun was about eight at this time, while his bride would have been not much older.

THE RESTORATION OF AMUN

Evidence suggests that Tutankhamun remained at **Akhet-aten** for the first three years of his reign before establishing his court at **Thebes**. Of course the boy king must in this period have been under the control of his **advisors**, who would have included **Nefertiti**, if she was still alive, as some believe she was, and cer-

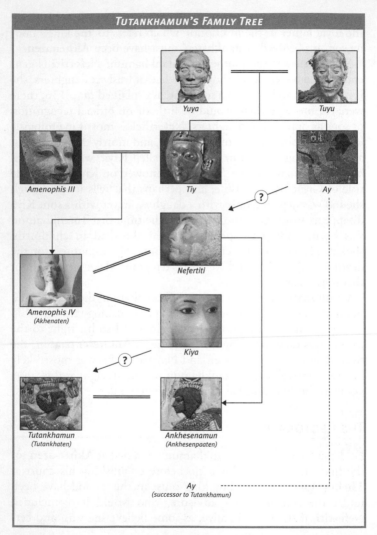

TUTANKHAMUN'S FAMILY TREE

Yuya

Tuyu

Amenophis III

Tiy

Ay

?

Nefertiti

Amenophis IV
(Akhenaten)

Kiya

?

Tutankhamun
(Tutankhaten)

Ankhesenamun
(Ankhesenpaaten)

Ay
(successor to Tutankhamun)

tainly the generals **Ay** and **Horemheb**, who had served under Akhenaten. Ay, who as perhaps the brother of queen Tiy was related to the new king, served Tutankhamun as vizier and held Yuya's old position of master of the cavalry, while Horemheb was commander of the army.

After the collapse of Atenism, Tutankhaten changed his name to Tutankhamun and was represented in the guise of the god Amun.

In this relief on the walls of Luxor Temple, carved there on the orders of Tutankhamun, dancers celebrate the Opet festival. Amun came to Luxor at such times to be with his divine harem.

At the prompting of his advisors, Tutankhamun moved towards **reinstating the traditional religious system** – and perhaps the move coincided with his ceremonial **coronation** by the **priests of Amun** at **Karnak**, an event depicted on some fragments of sculpture. The **Restoration Stele** issued in the king's name announced that 'the temples of the gods and goddesses, from the far south to the Delta, had fallen into decay, their sanctuaries were overgrown with weeds and their halls served as footpaths. Everything was in confusion. If a military expedition went to Syria, it met with no success. The gods had deserted Egypt and the prayers of the people had gone unanswered.' The reference to military operations in Syria probably indicates that the army, which had backed Akhenaten in his implementation of Atenism, had now withdrawn its support.

Tutankhamun, following the policy of Ay and the others, immediately took action to remedy this calamitous state of affairs.

He reopened the old temples, he rebuilt their sanctuaries, he reestablished their priesthoods and made lavish gifts to their treasuries, and he ordered that the effaced images of the old deities should be restored. But though Thebes was revived and regained its former splendour, those around Tutankhamun effectively prevented the god Amun from regaining his unique status by promoting other gods which were granted greater and nationwide importance. Among these, for example, was **Ptah**, the patron god of Memphis, a statuette of whom was included in Tutankhamun's tomb and is now included in the current exhibition. Nor did the king abandon his worship of the **Aten**, rather it was now one god among many. However, he did **change his name** from Tutankhaten – 'Living Image of Aten' – to Tutankhamun – 'Living Image of Amun'; while his wife, instead of being Ankhesenpaaten – 'She Lives Through Aten' – became **Ankhesnamun** – 'She Lives Through Amun'.

Work was resumed on monuments left unfinished by Amenophis III – most conspicuously the entrance corridor of **Luxor Temple**, where Tutankhamun caused reliefs to be carved along the walls showing the **Opet festival** and depicting **Amun** with **Mut** and **Khonsu**, accompanied by the pharoah and the priests on their voyage from Karnak at the height of the inundation season. Crowds of people follow by land, and there are scenes of rejoicing, of musicians and dancers, and of sacrifice. There was much truth in these scenes of popular celebration, for the reaction in favour of Amun was sustained less by the priesthood than by the common people.

DAYS OF THE KING

The royal couple lived, it seems, in the **former palace of Amenophis III** on the west bank of the Nile at Thebes, with its lake where queen Tiy used to sail on her barge called 'Aten

This gilded wooden statue of Tutankhamun depicts him aboard a papyrus boat hunting with a spear in the marshes.

Gleams'. Research into the contents of sealed jars found by Howard Carter shows that the king and queen were supplied with wine from estates in the Western Delta – red wine, specifically.

But this was not the king's only residence, and Tutankhamun probably spent much of his time at **Memphis**, which was the administrative capital of the country, though Thebes remained the nominal capital of Egypt. For example the inscription on the **ostrich feather fan** in the current exhibition indicates that the feathers were obtained by the king himself while **hunting** in the desert east of Heliopolis. According to one representation, Ankhesenamun would accompany her husband on duck shoots, handing him his arrows, and pointing out a particularly fat duck she fears he may overlook. In another, which appears on the back of the throne, she anoints her husband with perfume. She is a graceful figure, and a great tenderness is displayed between the couple in true Amarna style.

Twice Ankhesenamun became pregnant, and twice her **babies were stillborn**. True to the habit of her family, they were girls; both were mummified, and later they were deposited with the body of her husband in his tomb.

Though scenes on his tomb furniture show Tutankhamun **riding into battle in a chariot**, the revolutionary war machine of its age, he was almost certainly too young to have led any **military expeditions** personally. But he did send **Horemheb** to Palestine and Lebanon, where he bolstered the morale of allied princes who had remained loyal to Egypt in the face of a new enemy. The Mitanni – the enemies during the reigns of Amenophis III and Akhenaten – had been replaced by the **Hittites** who before the end of Tutankhamun's reign had conquered the Mitanni.

AKHET-ATEN AND THE VALLEY OF THE KINGS

The departure of the court and the loss of its patronage must have had a deleterious effect on the local economy at **Akhet-aten**, and

The possible remains of Akhenaten were found in Tomb 55 in the Valley of the Kings after being removed from Akhet-aten, perhaps on Tutankhamun's orders, but where later his coffin was viciously attacked.

as the place declined and its population dwindled, the decision was taken to remove the bodies of Akhenaten, Tiy and others of the royal family from their rock cut tombs in the cliffs above Amarna and transfer them to the **Valley of the Kings**. Thirty-three centuries later Theodore Davis would discover the ransacked **Tomb 55** in the Valley – probably a tomb for queen Tiy, whose mummy had been removed by the priests but whose golden shrine lay about in pieces, and for her son Akhenaten, his mummy case looking as if it had been furiously hacked and gouged to destroy its owner's identity.

Throughout Tutankhamun's reign the administration of affairs was in the hands of his vizier, **Ay**. Among his official duties would have been the **construction of a tomb** and a **mortuary temple** for his royal master. But the small tomb in which Tutankhamun was buried was almost certainly not meant for him, but probably for Ay himself, who because of his high services to the crown would have been granted burial in the Valley of the Kings – like Yuya and Tuyu, who may have been Ay's parents. In turn the far grander tomb in the Valley of the Kings in which Ay eventually installed himself must originally have been intended for Tutankhamun. Similarly, while Ay failed to get round to building a mortuary temple for his king, he did appropriate two statues of Tutankhamun which had been intended for it and, after a quick make-over, he placed them in his own mortuary temple in the Theban necropolis at **Medinet Habu**.

The Death of Tutankhamun

WHO KILLED THE KING?

Who or what killed the king? Nothing in the tomb gives an answer, except perhaps the **body of the king** itself. There are theories that he was murdered – poisoned, bludgeoned over the head, or even hanged. We will examine the evidence in the chapter 'Mysteries of Tutankhamun', following. Here is the straight story: what we know of his death, and the events that followed.

AN UNEXPECTED DEATH

Ay's behaviour over the tomb and the mortuary temple may seem to put him in a poor light, but he may have been only acting practically, when faced with the **unexpected death** of the young king, to preserve what he could of Akhenaten's legacy and the dynastic line that had been represented by Tutankhamun. Ay had been an enthusiastic adherent of Atenism, as we know from his unused tomb at Akhet-aten with its doorway inscribed with the Hymn to the Sun, and probably he was also related to the royal family. But there were others, led by **Horemheb**, who were no longer sympathetic, if they ever had been, and the court was divided between the two. However, at the moment of Tutankhamun's death, Horemheb was away to the north, fighting the Hittites in Syria, and by acting quickly, Ay would be able to replace the king himself before Horemheb returned.

Of **Ankhesenamun's fate** after her husband's death, nothing is known with certainty, and even her tomb, if it survives, has not been found. Perhaps she was among the very last people to leave Tutankhamun's tomb before Carter entered it 3300 years later, and to her attaches a romantic tale. 'I have no son, and my husband is dead,' Ankhesenamun is said to have written to the Hittite king. 'Send me a son of yours and I will make him king.' The story, as Carter unfolds it, goes that Ankhesenamun found herself faced with the political ambitions and, possibly, nuptial intentions of Ay. In answer to her letter, **Suppiluliumas**, far off in the Hittite capital of Hattusas in central Asia Minor, sent one of his sons to be Ankhesenamun's husband and rule as pharaoh. But, as a later Hittite text informs us, 'They killed him as they were conducting him to Egypt.' Who killed him, we do not know. Ay, who became the beneficiary of two deaths and hastily installed Tutankhamun in his small tomb? Or Horemheb, whose soldiers would likely have intercepted the Hittite prince as he entered the territory of an Egyptian ally in Palestine, Lebanon or Syria? Or was the letter-writer Nefertiti, still plotting after all these years? Or was it Meritaten, as some other scholars have suggested?

At any rate, in the grand tradition of Theban royal women who would only marry kings, one of them wrote a letter to Suppiluliumas, whose son was killed on his way to Egypt – and that in itself is one of those fascinating might-have-beens of history, the possibility of a marriage alliance between the two great superpowers of their day. Instead, nearly a century of enmity followed the murder of the Hittite prince.

A single piece of evidence – a **finger ring** inscribed with the names of Ankhesenamun and Ay – points to Ay having married Tutankhamun's queen to legitimise his rule, but if so then it would seem to have been a purely formal arrangement that lasted no more than four years. Ay's original wife, **Tiye**, who had been Nefertiti's nurse, is the only consort to appear among the decorations of Ay's tomb.

THE STRANGE CONTENTS OF TUTANKHAMUN'S TOMB

Against this historical backdrop of heresy, death and politics there is an intriguing question that needs an answer. How did Ay fill Tutankhamun's tomb so quickly, if the young king died with such sudden unexpectedness that there was no time to prepare a proper tomb? The answer is that the **treasures of Tutankhamun** are mostly the treasures of his ancestors, with as many as 80 percent of the core **burial goods** – those associated with the body – having been **recycled** from their original uses.

Tutankhamun's beautifully carved sarcophagus as seen in his burial chamber today. At its corners stand the four protective goddesses, Isis (left), Nephthys (foreground), Neith and Selkis. But it seems to have been meant for someone else and was recycled.

Close observation of the treasures provides a variety of conclusive evidence. Names have been altered, coffinettes reinscribed; some of the figures have female faces; some faces are not in the style normally used for Tutankhamun; the second of the four shrines had its cartouches replaced; and the sarcophagus bears traces of an earlier text. Most startling of all is that a new face was inserted in the magnificent **golden burial mask**. The original face was cut out and replaced with Tutankhamun's; even the soldering marks are visible. And on the outermost coffin, the wig resembles those seen on Akhenaten, but the face is Tutankhamun's, suggesting that the coffin had originally been made for Akhenaten. This would explain the mysterious **Tomb 55** in the Valley of the Kings, the one in which Tutankhamun deposited the remains of his father and grandmother after removing them from Akhet-aten. This was subsequently ransacked by robbers or vandals – but well before then, it was Ay's **source for the recycled grave goods** that were put to use in Tutankhamun's tomb.

REWRITING HISTORY: FROM AY TO RAMSES II

With the death of Tutankhamun and the disappearance of his widow Ankhesenamun the royal line was completely exhausted, so that Egypt experienced a run of commoner kings – **Ay** and **Horemheb** who concluded the 18th Dynasty, and **Ramses I**, the founder of the **19th Dynasty**, whose son Seti I and grandson Ramses II were both born before he was made king. These first three Ramessids were acutely aware of their origins, which perhaps explains their heightened need to legitimise their rule by obeisance to Amun. The initial stage of the **restoration of Amun** had been gradual, but it became more radical when Horemheb was king, while under Seti I and particularly Ramses II, all traces of Aten, and of Akhenaten and his immediate successors, were wiped out completely.

Seti I is shown in raised relief on the wall of his Gallery of Kings at his temple at Abydos. The names of almost every pharaoh from the 1st Dynasty onwards is recorded on the wall, but not the names of the heretic Akhenaten nor his successors Tutankhamun and Ay.

The full force of the **counter revolution against Atenism** proved to be more ferocious than anything that had been done by Akhenaten. **Seti I** continued Horemheb's work of restoring the old temples, and he also began the active persecution of the memory of Akhenaten, removing his name and those of his immediate successors from the records. He further reacted to the Amarna period by reverting to Old Kingdom artistic canons, decorating his works at Abydos and Thebes with finely cut and delicately coloured raised reliefs of exquisite if orthodox taste. Seti I and his son **Ramses II** set out to restore royal prestige by means of their **Asian campaigns** whose booty ensured accommodation with the Amun priesthood, though the longer term effect was to create a priesthood of such power and wealth that it rivalled the kings of the succeeding 20th Dynasty with a priestly dynasty of its own which ultimately secured control over Upper Egypt.

Ramses II made a point of **flattening Akhet-aten**, and the site was never built on again. The lengths to which Ramses went shows that Akhenaten in fact survived in popular memory for at least a century after his death and probably far longer than that. The destruction of Akhet-aten was part of his erasure, the erasing of his name everywhere, which to the Egyptian mind meant oblivion.

The approach of that oblivion would have been witnessed by **Ankhesenamun** in her widowhood as she saw Horemheb erase the memory of her husband by usurping his monuments, among them Tutankhamun's restoration stela and his Opet reliefs at Luxor Temple. But Horemheb and his successors left unharmed her husband's tomb, leaving it for a resolute archaeologist and his enlightened patron to pursue the search when the chances of success seemed too remote to justify the time and expense – recovering Tutankhamun and making him spectacularly famous after more than three thousand years, and leaving us with the continuing mystery of his story.

Mysteries of Tutankhamun

'A WELL SET STAGE FOR DRAMATIC HAPPENINGS'

What really did happen, back in about 1327 BC, when Tutankhamun died? The evidence is that his death came suddenly and unexpectedly. But why did he die so young? From the outset there were suggestions of dark motives, with Howard Carter offering a speculation of his own:

> It was Ay who was largely responsible for establishing the boy king upon the throne. Quite possibly he had designs upon it himself already, but, not feeling secure enough for the moment, preferred to bide his time and utilise the opportunities he would undoubtedly have, as minister to a young and inexperienced sovereign, to consolidate his position. It is interesting to speculate, and when we remember that Ay in his turn was supplanted by another of the leading officials of Akhenaten's reign, the General Horemheb, and that neither of them had any real claim to the throne, we can be reasonbly sure that in this little by-way of history there was a well set stage for dramatic happenings.

Since then there has been no lack of **theories about the death of Tutankhamun**, about how and why he was murdered – and by whom.

INVESTIGATIONS OF TUTANKHAMUN'S MUMMY

Since the discovery of his tomb in November 1922, Tutankhamun's **mummified remains** have been subject to repeated examinations. The first was a **post mortem** carried out in 1925 by a British and an Egyptian doctor in the presence of Carter and assembled archaeologists and Egyptian officials. In 1968 Tutankhamun was **X-rayed** for the first time, and then again in 1978. Finally early in 2005 Tutankhamun was once more disinterred, though not removed from the burial chamber, and was exposed to a full-blown **CT scan**, a state of the art technique which enormously improves on the results of X-ray technology.

With each of these investigations something new was learnt about Tutankhamun, about his physical condition in life, about how he might have died, about the ancient embalming process he

Tutankhamun's hand, his fingers sheathed in gold, was severed from his arm at the time of the 1925 post mortem. Indeed he was decapitated and his entire body was dismembered.

underwent, and about his treatment by the examiners themselves since the discovery of his tomb. Some questions have been answered, but new ones have arisen, and the process has generated yet more theories and controversy – though the CT scan of 2005 has probably taken the forensic investigation into the fate of Tutankhamun as far as it can go. Now let us review the case.

THE POST MORTEM OF 1925

Tutankhamun's post mortem began on **11 November 1925** in the presence of Howard Carter, members of the Antiquities Department and Egyptian government officials. The autopsy lasted for eight days and was performed by **Professor Douglas Derry** of Cairo University's medical school, who had long experience of examining royal mummies for the Egyptian Museum in Cairo, and **Dr Saleh Bey Hamdi**, the Egyptian Health Inspector. At this point the mummy was still in its innermost solid gold coffin from which it could not be removed without risk of damage, owing to the fragile and powdery nature of the outer wrappings and a pitch-like substance that had gathered underneath the body and glued it to its gold surround. At each stage photographs were taken by **Harry Burton**, showing the removal of layers of wrappings and the 97 funerary objects that had been bound in with the mummy. On 19 November the two physicians declared the examination complete.

Tutankhamun had been not only unwrapped but decapitated and **dismembered** in the process, and Carter indicated his regret by issuing a statement on behalf of the team that X-ray analysis had proved impossible as the gold coffin and the thick pitch-like material were impervious to the rays. Derry and Hamdi had detached Tutankhamun's head and limbs from his trunk, and his torso from the pelvis. They separated his arms at the elbows, his legs at the knees, and they severed his hands and feet from their limbs. In fact this was the only way that various objects like rings,

Beneath his golden mask and his royal diadem, Tutankhamun wore a skullcap which could not be removed as it was stuck to his head with pitch. The pattern is an Amarna design, showing that at the time of his death the worship of Aten had not yet been proscribed.

bracelets and pendents could be removed from the body, or indeed that the gold mask, which was held fast to Tutankhamun's head by pitch, could be prised off. A bit of ear was detached when the royal diadem was removed.

In his report, Derry concluded that from the evidence of his lower limbs, Tutankhamun had been **nineteen years old** at the time of his death. But apart from noting a lesion on his cheek which was healing when he died, he could throw no light on the cause of the young king's death. Tutankhamun was then reassembled on a sand tray and returned to his outermost gilded wood coffin, which was returned to the brown quartzite sarcophagus left in place in the burial chamber.

THE 1968 X-RAY EXAMINATION

Because Tutankhamun had been removed from his coffin and unwrapped, it was practicable for his body to be X-rayed. In **1968** a team led by **Ronald Harrison**, professor of anatomy at Liverpool University, was permitted to disinter Tutankhamun for the express purpose of **X-raying the body** to determine the cause of the boy king's premature death.

Harrison's examination revealed the way in which Tutankhamun's body had been treated by its ancient Egyptian **embalmers**. The broad, flat-topped and longish skull was found to be empty, the **brain** having been removed in the embalming process, except for two thick deposits of opaque material, probably solidified liquid resin which had likely been injected into the skull cavity through the nasal passage. One of these deposits was at the back of the skull, as would naturally have occurred with the king's corpse lying on its back when the resin was injected. But the other deposit was at the top of the skull, which could only mean that the king had been suspended upside down when a second dose of resin was introduced.

Notwithstanding this commonsense explanation, people in search of a sensational theory took the thickening within the skull as evidence of a **heavy blow to Tutankhamun's head**, which seemed confirmed when the X–ray also revealed a loose fragment of bone within the cranium, leading to the claim that **Tutankhamun had been murdered**.

The X-rays also revealed that the sternum and the frontal rib cage were missing, presumably removed at the same time as Tutankhamun's internal organs. This feature had been missed in the 1925 post mortem because the **mummy's chest** was thickly pasted over with hardened resin and embedded with minute fragments from a beaded floral collar which Carter and his medical team did not attempt to move. Had the young king's chest been crushed in some accident, resulting in his death? He was often represented as a keen sportsman, and one suggestion was that Tutankhamun might have been **hunting in his chariot** with the reins wrapped about himself to leave his hands free for the use of javelin, boomerang or bow, when the chariot keeled over and he was dragged along beneath the wheels.

One theory says that Tutankhamun died when he was dragged beneath the wheels of his hunting chariot – which if true would add an ironic poignancy to the presence of chariots in his tomb.

Finally Harrison discovered that Tutankhamun's penis was missing, though it was there in a photograph taken by Burton in 1926. Speculation immediately arose that it had been snapped off by some collector as a mantlepiece trophy.

Following Harrison's examination the corpse was reinterred a second time, still resting on the sand tray placed within the original outer coffin.

MORE X-RAYS: 1978

Because Harrison's X-rays turned out to be of little use for examining the state of Tutankhamun's **teeth**, an American orthodontist and royal mummy expert, **James E. Harris**, was granted permission to disinter the body for a third time in **1978**. This one-day session showed that Tutankhamun's condition had deteriorated; his eye sockets had collapsed and his right ear was missing. Also his body was noticeably darker; apparently the result of combustion caused by the various oils and fats attendant on the mummification process and in combination with exposure to air, light and heat.

CT SCAN IN 2005

Early in **2005**, **Zahi Hawass**, head of Egypt's Supreme Council for Antiquities, decided to answer the continuing questions and theories concerning the demise of Tutankhamun by subjecting the mummy to a **CT** (computed topography) **scan**, a sophisticated kind of X-ray which records not only bone but tissue too, and which can be used to build up a three-dimensional image of the entire body. The same technology had revealed that Oetzi, the 5200-year-old hunter-gatherer found preserved in an Alpine glacier, had been shot in the shoulder with an arrow and had a fresh gash on his hand. For weeks the anticipation mounted – as perhaps it was meant to mount, giving worldwide publicity to the

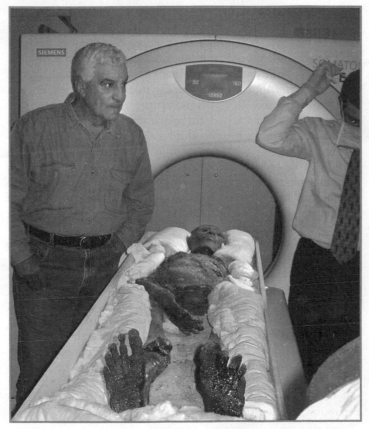

Dr Zahi Hawass, secretary general of Egypt's Supreme Council of Antiquities, supervises the CT scan of Tutankhamun, which to minimise disturbance to his body was conducted within his tomb.

new Tutankhamun exhibition – before Hawass announced the final result in March: 'We don't know how the king died, but we are now sure it was not murder. Maybe he died on his own. The case is closed. We should not disturb the king any more'.

According to the report by the all-Egyptian team, the CT scan, which was performed in the burial chamber of Tutankhamun's tomb in January 2005, found no evidence of a blow to the back of Tutankhamun's head and no other evidence of foul play. Likewise the bone fragments in Tutankhamun's skull were blamed on careless embalmers or on the Egyptian and British doctors who performed the 1925 post mortem.

Some team members said Tutankhamun may have died after a **serious accident** in which his **thigh snapped** after a fall or forceful blow, leaving a gaping wound which became infected. 'Although the break itself would not have been life-threatening, infection might have set in,' the report said. 'However, it is also possible, although less likely, that this fracture was caused by the embalmers.' Indeed less likely, as the presence of embalming fluid in the wound suggests that it was present before death. The fracture seems to have been made days before the king died because there are no clear signs that the wound healed.

Happily, the team also found **Tutankhamun's penis**; it had been there all along, admittedly not in the usual spot; rather it had dropped off into the sand-filled tray. Also happily, perhaps, for those who hold out for a murder conspiracy, come the remarks of **Ashraf Selim**, executive director of the Cairoscan Centre. Tutankhamun's CT-scan was 'relatively limited', he said. 'Even though the possibility of his having been killed by a blow to the back of the head has now been proven wrong, we are still not sure that Tutankhamun's death was natural. He could have been murdered with poison.'

4. Tombs and Afterlife

The Valley of the Kings and Mummification

Carter's first sight of the sealed door of the golden shrine containing Tutankhamun's sarcoghagus

The Egyptian Afterlife

THE VARIETIES OF RELIGIOUS BELIEF

An ever-present characteristic of ancient Egyptian religion was its readiness to hold a variety of beliefs simultaneously, though the emphasis might change from period to period. There were deities in wholly animal or human form, others with animal heads and human bodies, while cosmic phenomena such as the stars and sun could be deities too. Moreover they might combine or be elaborated or borrow attributes from one another; they were like energy fields that could operate independently or together, and unlike the modern conception of an otherworldly god they manifested themselves in plants, animals, cult objects, statues and in the king himself.

Yet for all their permutations and bewildering variety their names and images can be traced from the beginnings of ancient Egyptian history to its end. They were the expression of an unbroken cultural identity whose most fundamental belief was that behind the apparent flux of this world, behind birth, decay and death, there was a **changeless essence**, an eternal blessedness, for which all Egyptians longed. One belief did not exclude the others. In fact the Egyptians spoke of their gods as numbering in the millions and never attempted to catalogue them all. Some were associated with the king and state, their worship guarded from profane eyes by the priesthoods; others were associated with magical medicine and the

This vegetating Osiris was found in Tutankhamun's tomb. A tray in the form of Osiris, god of fertility and lord of the underworld, was filled with Nile silt and planted with seeds which were expected to sprout inside the sealed tomb as a symbol of rebirth.

multitudinous needs of daily life and were venerated by the population at large; and some, like the cult of the ancient fertility god **Osiris**, ultimately extended throughout all levels of society.

The one great exception to this plurality of belief was the **heresy of Akhenaten** and his worship of one god exclusively, the **Aten** or sun disc. Tutankhamun was born into this heresy, and it was as he was emerging from it, or perhaps was refusing to abandon it, that he died so suddenly and so young.

Taking it with you: the development of Tombs

Already in about 4500 BC – some fifteen centuries before the unification of Upper and Lower Egypt and the start of the 1st Dynasty – Egyptians were buried in a contracted position facing west, which in Dynastic times would become associated with the **Land of the Dead**. The pottery bowls and the clay and ivory figurines they took to their graves indicate a developed belief in the **afterlife** – one they had no intention of entering empty-handed.

During the **Early Dynastic Period** – that is during the 1st and 2nd Dynasties (c3000 to 2686 BC) – ordinary Egyptians were buried in **pits** dug in the sand, but for people of rank a large pit was cut from the bedrock and divided into **chambers**, and a rectangular single storey flat-roofed mud brick structure called a **mastaba** was built atop it, and this too was divided into chambers which were filled with **grave goods** to see them through eternity.

In Early Dynastic times kings ruled with absolute authority as gods, and in death they expected to be worshipped as gods. Therefore apart from having more imposing tombs, kings also had separate **funerary shrines** where rites could be performed. Moreover, to ensure the continuation of the absolute authority they enjoyed in life, 1st Dynasty kings took everything with them at death: royal burials were accompanied by **sacrificial humans** – probably officials, priests, servants and women from the royal household, who were strangled with the intention that they should continue to offer the king their services in the afterlife. Also lions were sometimes sacrificed to provide the king with game for hunting, as were dwarfs to keep the king amused. Human sacrifice, however, must have had something of a dispiriting effect on the royal court; in any case, the practice was abandoned by the beginning of the 2nd Dynasty.

Even so, throughout their history the ancient Egyptians' view of the afterlife, whatever its spiritual component, continued to be expressed in material and literal terms: they intended to carry on physically as they had before. Already during the 2nd Dynasty high officials had elaborate tombs which amounted to entire **houses for the afterlife**, the largest discovered having twenty-seven rooms and containing men's and women's quarters with bathrooms and toilets.

But it was impossible to enter the afterlife, the ancient Egyptians believed, unless a **body was preserved**. This had previously occurred naturally, from the dehydrating effects of burial in the sand; now the growing fashion among the better off for burial in wooden coffins required that their bodies be wrapped in resin-soaked linen if they were not to decompose (see the chapter following, on Mummification).

THE MEANING OF PYRAMIDS

The **Step Pyramid** built for Djoser (c2667–c2648 BC), second king of the 3rd Dynasty, marked the beginning of a new pyramidal form that was to be explored to its limits during the first century of the Old Kingdom. Its architect was Djoser's vizier Imhotep, who was also Chief of the Observers, the title borne by the high priest at what the Greeks would later call **Heliopolis** (City of the Sun), now overbuilt by the northern suburbs of Cairo. But in Imhotep's time **star cults** were probably pre-eminent at Heliopolis, his title referring to astronomical observations generally and not yet to a cult of the sun. Symbolically the Step Pyramid was the means by which Djoser could ascend to the heavens and commune there, a star among eternal stars.

Whether **true pyramids** with smoothly sloping sides, first built by Sneferu (c2613-c2589 BC), the first king of the 4th Dynasty, evolved naturally out of the earlier stepped form or were induced by a change in religion is not known, but certainly the two ideas were to coincide. For the sun cult eventually became predominant at Heliopolis, where it was associated with the **creation myth** of the primal hill which bearing the sun god Ra rose from the chaos of the waters, just as after the Nile's annual inundation the waters subsided and the sun drew the harvest from the mud. Heliopolis also claimed a primal hill, the **benben**, a word whose root was bound up with the notion of shining and ascending. The *benben* had already been depicted in 2nd Dynasty inscriptions; now, in Sneferu's time, it was manifested architecturally in the form of a true pyramid, at once symbolising the reborn sun rising above the land and the rebirth of the king himself.

On the Giza plateau, king **Cheops** (c2589–c2566 BC) would build the greatest pyramid of all, and his successors Cephren and Mycerinus would further emphasise the connection between solar worship and royal rule by incorporating the name of the sun god **Ra** into their names (Khafra and Menkaura in the Egyptian versions), a practice that would recur throughout the rest of ancient Egyptian history. Autocratic power, however, was still in their hands, and their **pyramids at Giza** were at least as much an assertion of their authority as a symbol of the sun cult.

THE CULTS OF RA AND OSIRIS

Things would change with **Userkaf** (c2494–c2487 BC) who before ascending the throne as the first king of the 5th Dynasty had most

The naked figure of the goddess Nut was often depicted in burial chambers in the Valley of the Kings. Here she swallows the sun which travels down the length of her body to be reborn at dawn.

likely been high priest at Heliopolis, and it was now that the **cult of Ra** was raised to the official state religion. Userkaf and his 5th Dynasty successors all built modest pyramids, but most also diverted considerable resources to building elaborate sun temples. This represented a significant transfer of power and wealth to the priesthood of Ra, for it meant a multiplication of guardians and priests who were sustained by a rising level of royal donations and by endowments of land exempted from taxation in perpetuty.

Neither Unas (c2375-c2345 BC), the last king of the 5th Dynasty, nor his two immediate predecessors built sun temples, though not because the cult of the sun was waning. The explanation is forthcoming inside the pyramid of Unas at Saqqara where the walls of his tomb chamber are covered with hieroglyphic inscriptions, the **Pyramid Texts**, which are the earliest extensive mortuary literature of Egypt. The Pyramid Texts identify the deceased king with **Osiris**, lord of the underworld and originally a god of vegetation and fertility, whose ancient cult had been incorporated by the Heliopolitan priests into their solar theology by the end of the 5th Dynasty.

Osiris was said to have been born of the sky goddess **Nut**, who in turn was the creation of the sun god. Her naked figure arching across the heavens represented the sun god's vision of an ordered firmament, so that he would be swallowed by her at sundown and then emerge from her vulva at dawn.

Nut is described in the Pyramid Texts as enfolding the dead pharaoh in her soul, a euphemism for him being placed in his **sarcophagus**. The practice of burial in a stone sarcophagus began with Cheops in the previous dynasty, and subsequently it became common not only for kings but also for lesser mortals to be placed in a sarcophagus whose interior was carved with the naked figure of Nut. The deceased, in being symbolically enclosed by Nut to await rebirth, was therefore associating himself with ancient Egypt's two greatest cults, those of the sun and of Osiris.

The **Osiris cult** had a humanising effect on Egyptian theology and society. A king had previously felt himself to be a god, absolute in his powers; subsequently his authority was shared with Ra, though the sun god was also a guarantor of his royal position. Just as in this life ordinary Egyptians were totally dependent on the favour of the king, so likewise their entry into the afterlife also depended on the agency of the king. Osiris, however, as lord of the underworld, performed the role of a **judge** who examined the souls of the dead and condemned those unfit for the afterlife – so that now even the king had to plead his case.

With the rise of the cult of Osiris came the egalitarian notion of a **personal god** from whom king and commoners alike sought **redemption**.

THE BOOK OF THE DEAD

By the time Amosis I established the 18th Dynasty and with it the New Kingdom in about 1550 BC, Egyptians had well developed ideas about the **afterlife**, which they conceived of as an extension of their present lives. **The Book of the Dead**, which first appeared at this time, was effectively a traveller's guide to the beyond: it told you how to get there, and what to expect once you had arrived. For a king the promise was that he would take his place in the divine cosmic cycle. For lesser people the expectation was a comfortable home and a parcel of land, larger or smaller according to one's social standing. Both king and commoner could expect a warm welcome to the afterlife by the gods, with the promise of remaining among them for all eternity. But the question was how to get there.

An important element in the passage to the afterlife was the **judgement of the dead**. The conduct of the deceased was assessed by weighing the heart in a balance against the **feather of Maat**, the goddess of truth and justice, in the presence of Osiris.

A vignette in the Book of the Dead illustrates the scene: the dead man stands on one side, Maat on the other, and between them the jackal-headed **Anubis** holds the balance, while next to him the result is recorded by **Thoth**, the scribe of the gods. Behind Thoth crouches a terrible monster with the head of a crocodile, the forequarters of a lion and the hindquarters of a hippopotamus. Its name is **Ammit**, which means 'Eater of the Dead', and his function was to devour the hearts of those who failed the test. But in fact Ammit went forever hungry; the Book of the Dead contained both the questions and the answers that determined whether the heart would outweigh the feather, and so carefully was it studied by the prospective dead that not a single instance is recorded in Egyptian literature of the deceased failing the test. Instead everyone was welcomed by Osiris as the 'blessed dead'.

While lesser people perused the Book of the Dead in papyrus form, kings had it painted on the walls of their tombs, though sparingly, with far more space taken up by specialist navigational guides reserved for royalty, such as the **Amduat** (also known as *The Book Of What Is In The Underworld*) and the **Book of Gates**. In Tutankhamun's burial chamber, for example, the Amduat is painted on the west wall where it shows the **solar boat** and below it **twelve baboons**, representing the twelve hours of the night. Like the sun, the king must voyage through the darkness before achieving rebirth at dawn.

AFTERLIFE MAINTENANCE

Notwithstanding this all but certain entry to the afterlife, nor even the promise of house and plot of land, the deceased required the services of his family and friends in this world to sustain him in the next. This meant that the **funerary rituals** had to be performed and his **mortuary cult** had to be kept up. Those with families of wealth and standing could expect extensive and lavish attentions, but what really mattered was the ritual itself and the power of the spoken word, and provided these were performed correctly, even the poorest and most humble person could expect to be received and sustained in the afterlife.

Yet the ancient Egyptians never abandoned their habit of seeing life and the afterlife in physical and literal terms, and so another condition for survival in the afterlife was the **integrity of the dead person's body**, which could not be allowed to decompose, and for security had to be sealed away in a tomb.

Mummification

THE INTEGRITY OF THE DEAD

Mummification began in about 2900 BC as a substitute for the natural process of dessication that occurred when a body was buried in the sand. Bodies buried in tombs were wrapped in resin-soaked linen in an attempt to prevent them from decomposing. But it was only around the beginning of the 18th Dynasty that successful techniques were developed for preserving the body.

NEW KINGDOM EMBALMING

The largest collection of Egyptian mummies is, not surprisingly, in the Egyptian Museum in Cairo. Here, one of the earliest examples is the **mummified body of Sekenenra** – a mummy that illustrates the problems of preservation.

Sekenenra was the penultimate king of the 17th Dynasty and probably the father of Amosis I, the first king of the 18th Dynasty. In about 1555 BC Sekenenra died violently from an axe wound to the forehead and a dagger blow to the back of the neck, probably in the heat of battle against the Hyksos. As a consequence of the king's sudden and violent death on the battlefield, the embalming of the corpse seems to have been hastily carried out. The viscera were extracted through a cut in the left side of the abdomen and the cavity was filled with linen, but no treatment of the badly damaged head was attempted, and the brain was left in place. Most of the flesh has subsequently disappeared from the mummy, leaving a skeleton within a thin covering of decaying skin.

The height of the embalming process was achieved only in about 1000 BC, that is after the collapse of the New Kingdom, but the Egyptian Museum does have a famous collection of pharaohs and their ladies from the 18th and 19th Dynasties, among them **Amenophis I**, **Tuthmosis II**, **Tuthmosis IV**, **Seti I** and **Ramses II**, all of them fairly well preserved – indeed, any apparent deficiencies are less due to the embalming process or to being put on public view, than to the ransacking of their bodies by tomb robbers in ancient times.

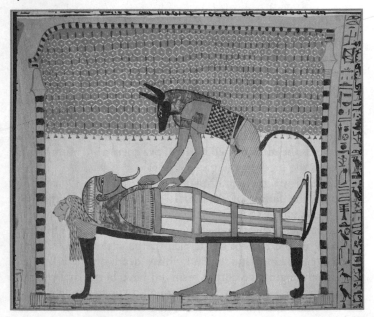

Tomb workers in the Valley of the Kings lived nearby at Deir el Medina where they decorated their own tombs with a particular knowledge of the funerary arts. Here jackal-headed Anubis, a god associated with interment, is performing his craft on the deceased.

Traditionally during the 18th Dynasty, seventy days passed between the death and funeral. First the **internal organs** were removed through an incision in the left side of the body, and these were put in four containers known as **Canopic jars**. Kings and other important figures might have their brains removed. This was done by cutting the septum, the cartilege which divides the nostrils, and then withdrawing the brain in bits and pieces through the nose. More usually, however, the brain was left inside the skull; only around 1000 BC did it become common practice to remove it.

The most important part of the embalming process was the **dehydration of the body**, which was achieved by soaking it in a bath of **natrun**, a naturally occurring mineral compounded of sodium carbonate and sodium bicarbonate. Resins, oils, myrrh and incense might then be applied, but they were less essential for the desired result, and indeed an excess of unguents could be counterproductive and

Tutankhamun after the 1925 post mortem. Notice that his penis is still in place.

promote decomposition. Finally the body was elaborately wrapped in **linen bandages**.

THE FULL MENU

Not only royalty and the nobility were mummified but all classes of ancient Egyptian society, subject to their ability to pay. The best contemporary account of mummification comes from the Greek historian **Herodotus**, who visited Egypt in the mid-5th century BC. He noted the varieties of mummification on offer from embalmers in his day, which was probably not much different to what had been available during the 18th Dynasty a thousand years before.

The embalmers, when a body is brought to them, produce three specimen models in wood, painted to resemble nature, and graded in quality. After pointing out the differences in quality, they ask which of the three is required, and the kinsmen of the dead man, having agreed upon a price, go away and leave the embalmers to their work.

The most perfect process is as follows: as much as possible of the brain is extracted through the nostrils with an iron hook, and what the hook cannot reach is rinsed out with drugs. Next the flank is laid open with a flint knife and the whole contents of the abdomen is removed. The cavity is then throughly cleansed and washed out, first with palm wine and again with an infusion of pounded spices. After that it is filled with pure bruised myrrh, cassia and every other aromatic substance with the exception of frankincense and sewn up again, after which the body is placed in natrun for seventy days. When this period, which must not be exceeded, is over, the body is washed and then wrapped from head to foot in linen cut into strips and smeared on the under side with gum. In this condition the body is given back to the family, who have a wooden case made, shaped like the human figure, into which it is put.

When, for reasons of expense, the second quality is called for, no incision is made and the intestines are not removed, but oil of cedar is injected into the body through the anus which is afterwards stopped up. The body is then pickled in natrun for the prescribed number of days, on the last of which the oil is drained off. The effect is so powerful that as it leaves the body it brings with it the stomach and intestines in a liquid state, and as the flesh, too, is dissolved by the natrun, nothing of the body is left but the bones and skin. After this treatment it is returned to the family without further fuss.

MODERN EMBALMING

On 5 April 2005 *The Times* of London reported that the body of Pope John Paul II had been treated by a family of Rome undertakers named the Signoraccis. The head of the company, Massimo Signoracci, who also teaches forensic pathology at Rome University, would only say that his family had 'always been proud to preserve the bodies of the Popes. It is a huge emotion to be near and work on someone so famous and loved.' His father and uncles had embalmed the bodies of Popes John XXIII in 1963 and both Paul VI and John Paul I in 1978. *The Times* report continued:

'Embalming, a practice that dates back to the Ancient Egyptians, traditionally involves not only the use of oils and herbs to preserve the bodies of the dead, but also the removal of the internal organs. The aim is partly aesthetic and partly to delay physical decay and to stop the spread of infection. The Signoraccis, like other modern undertakers, use a technique that involves removing blood and gases from the body and the insertion of a disinfecting fluid, usually through the carotid or femoral artery.

'In the past, the organs of dead Popes were removed and placed in jars in the Church of Saints Vincenzo and Anastasio near the Trevi Fountain in Rome, while their bodies were buried in the crypt of St Peter's. Leo XIII was the last Pope to be treated in this way when he died in 1903. Signor Signoracci confirmed that embalming techniques nowadays consisted of the intravenous injection of formaldehyde.'

The third method, used for embalming the bodies of the poor, is simply to clear out the intestines with a purge and keep the body seventy days in natrun. It is then given back to the family to be taken away.

When the wife of a distinguished man dies, or any woman who happens to be beautiful or well known, her body is not given to the embalmers immediately, but only after the lapse of three or four days. This is a precautionary measure to prevent the embalmers from violating the corpse, a thing which is said actually to have happened in the case of a woman who had just died. The culprit was given away by one of his fellow workmen.

The Valley of the Kings

THE SECRECY OF TOMBS

The practice followed in the Old and Middle Kingdoms of pharaohs constructing **mortuary temples** that also served as tombs was abruptly discontinued by Tuthmosis I (c1504–c1492), the third king of the 18th Dynasty. The pyramids of the past were all too obvious targets for tomb robbers, and the intention of Tuthmosis was to build a modest tomb in a secret and inaccessible place. Though his mortuary temple has never been found, he probably built it on the plain of the west bank of the Nile, while he was the first to have his **tomb** dug behind the Theban hills in one of the remotest arms of what became the royal necropolis – the **Valley of the Kings**.

It was probably not lost on Tuthmosis I or his successors that the highest peak of the Theban hills looms like a pyramid above both plain and Valley. The symbolism of sun worship was continued, even as the tombs dug deep into the underworld of Osiris. Tuthmosis also founded **Deir el Medina**, a community of craftsmen and necropolis workers, at the south end of the Theban hills, who would continue to build and decorate royal tombs throughout the New Kingdom, a period of 500 years. More than 62 tombs have been found so far, most of them dating from the 18th to 20th Dynasties.

Deir el Medina was founded for tomb workers by Tuthmosis I, the first pharaoh to be buried in the Valley of the Kings. The necropolis workers themselves were partial to building pyramid tombs in their back gardens.

SPACE CAPSULES

As the offerings to dead kings and their funerary rituals took place at their mortuary temples on the plain, their **tombs** were therefore isolated receptacles for the sarcophagus, and their decoration concentrated exclusively on the formulae efficacious in transferring the deceased from this world to the next. In fact the tombs in the Valley of the Kings are more like space capsules, vehicles expressly designed for the journey through the heavens and the underworld. A similar pattern of construction and decoration is followed in each of the tombs in the Valley of the Kings. Three **corridors** lead to an **antechamber** giving onto the **main hall** with its **sunken floor** for receiving the sarcophagus.

The tombs were cut into the soft limestone by two teams of twenty-five men working alternating ten-day shifts. They normally lived at Deir el Medina, but when on shift stayed in huts within the valley. Construction of a tomb began at the beginning

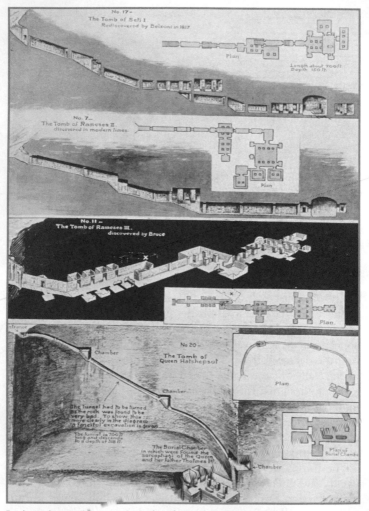

Ever larger, deeper and more complex tombs as featured in the Illustrated London News.

of a reign and never took more than six years to complete. Once the interior surfaces were prepared, the designs and inscriptions were sketched in black; the designs filled in; the hieroglyphics outlined in red; and the decorations carved and finally painted.

The dead pharaoh, absorbed in the sun god, sailed through the underworld at night in a boat, with enemies and dangers to be avoided along the way. This is the recurrent theme of the **tomb decorations**, the inscriptions being extensive quotations from the *Amduat* or *Book of the Underworld* and the *Book of the Gates* which provide instructions for charting the course; sometimes also the *Book of Day and Night*. Pictorially, there are three registers, the middle one showing the **river of passage**, the top and bottom registers depicting the **underworld shores** with their inhabitants of deities and demons. The registers are divided into 12 sections for the 12 hours of the night. After this nocturnal voyage the naked body of the goddess **Nut** gives birth each morning to the sun.

TOMB PECKING ORDERS

The size of a royal tomb was, in general, related to the length of a pharaoh's reign. Just as a pharaoh built or added his embellishments to temples, or claimed to extend the boundaries of the Egyptian empire, so each new pharaoh sought to outdo his predecessor by excavating a bigger tomb, longer and with more chambers, or with some new feature, or more decorations. The principle is illustrated by reviewing the tombs of those pharaohs whose grave goods are represented in the current exhibition: Amenophis II, Tuthmosis IV and Amenophis III.

The tomb of **Amenophis II** was found in 1898; it had been robbed in antiquity, and barely more than the sarcophagus remained, but the treasure must have been huge, for there are four large storerooms for funerary goods off the burial chamber, and it was in these that a few wooden figures were found, as well as several mummies of the 21st Dynasty who had been brought here by the priests for safekeeping after their own tombs had been vandalised. Only the burial chamber in Amenophis II's tomb was decorated, and then only in a sketchlike form, though the entire Amduat was represented.

Tuthmosis IV's tomb was discovered by Howard Carter in 1903. It has nine descending passages compared with seven in the tomb of Amenophis II, the sarcophagus is the largest to that date, and while the burial chamber was unfinished, the antechamber was decorated, no longer in the schematic form of previous tombs but with colourful paintings. An innovation found in the tomb were niches for magic bricks.

The tomb of **Amenophis III** was discovered by members of Napoleon's expedition and was the first 18th Dynasty tomb to be found, though it was first examined systematically by Carter in 1915. Far larger than anything constructed before in the Valley,

This scene on the wall of Tuthmosis III's burial chamber in the Valley of the Kings shows the veneration of a scarab which was associated with the sun's passage across the sky and with regeneration.

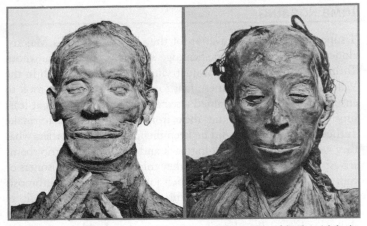

Yuya and Tuyu, though commoners, were privileged with a tomb in the Valley of the Kings. It helped that Yuya was an important military commander and that his daughter Tiy had married the king.

Amenophis' tomb has its burial chamber and antechamber covered in coloured paintings, which include for the first time depictions of the king's *ka* and the goddess Nut.

Tutankhamun's tomb was of course a great exception; it should have been sizeable, but instead it was miniature – but that is because he was buried in a hastily adapted tomb that had been intended for a courtier or official. The burial chamber of his tomb was decorated at the last moment, and then only in a rough and conventional manner, and with only enough space for abbreviated excerpts or suggestive motifs from the *Amduat*.

Very occasionally a non-royal personage was permitted burial in the Valley as a special honour – **Yuya** and **Tuyu**, the parents-in-law of Amenophis III, are the outstanding example: their tomb was the most celebrated find in the Valley of the Kings until Howard Carter discovered Tutankhamun's undisturbed burial chamber in 1922. But a tomb such as Yuya's and Tuyu's could not be decorated; that was a privilege reserved for royalty alone.

TOMB ROBBING

'I superintended the excavation of the cliff tomb of His Majesty, alone, no one seeing, no one hearing,' said Ineni, the official whom Tuthmosis I put in charge of quarrying the first royal tomb in the Valley of the Kings. But Ineni fails to tell us what steps he took to ensure that the work remained a secret. He must have had at least fifty men hewing out the rock from the mountain to make Tuthomosis' tomb; how did he keep them from telling others what they were doing, or from going back and robbing the tomb themselves? It has been suggested that they might have been prisoners of war, who were slaughtered after their job was done. But Tuthmosis himself had established the tomb workers' village of Deir el Medina, and its inhabitants were more likely to have been highly skilled and specially selected craftsmen, too valuable to squander. More likely they were paid very well and policed very well, and would have understood the ferocious punishments awaiting anyone caught tomb robbing – the ingenious tortures followed by a lingering death, most likely by impalement on a stake.

And yet the secret was not kept. Though the tomb overseen by Ineni was intended for Tuthmosis I, it was enlarged by his daughter Hatshepsut – and was that very same tomb which Howard Carter had explored with such difficulty in 1903, only to discover that it had been violated in ancient times. 'Strange sights the Valley must have seen,' reflected Carter:

And desperate the ventures that took place in it. One can imagine the plotting for days beforehand, the secret rendezvous on the cliff by night, the bribing or drugging of the cemetery guards, and then the desperate burrowing in the dark, the scramble through a small hole into the burial chamber, the hectic search by a glimmering light for treasure that was portable, and the return home at dawn laden with booty. We can imagine these things, and at the same time we can realise how inevitable it all was. By providing his mummy with the elaborate and costly outfit which he thought essential to its dignity, the king was himself compassing its destruction. The temptation was too great. Wealth beyond the dreams of avarice lay there at the disposal of whoever should find the means to reach it, and sooner or later the tomb robber was bound to win through.

Under the powerful pharaohs of the 18th and 19th Dynasties local officials were closely supervised and tomb looting was kept in check. But tombs were robbed under the weaker rulers of the **20th Dynasty**. A picture of surprising detail can be built up from surviving papyri of the necropolis workers at Deir el Medina enduring food shortages and late payment of wages, and riots, pay disputes and strikes. There are also documented accounts of bribery and collusion among workers, priests and officials. One papyrus describes a major Theban law case during the **reign of Ramses IX** in the 20th Dynasty in which the mayor of Thebes

Tomb 55 in the Valley of the Kings was one of those plundered and wrecked by tomb robbers. Queen Tiy had been transferred to the tomb from Amarna but was moved out again before the sacking.

brought to the vizier's attention stories of tomb robbing at the necropolis. The matter was investigated by the chief of the necropolis police and the stories were denied; the vizier then ensured that the mayor of Thebes was disgraced for making malicious and politically inspired accusations.

Some years later, however, as the tomb robbings continued, the case was reopened and it became clear that both the **vizier and the chief of police** were up to their eyeballs in corruption. After being beaten with rods on his feet and hands to assist his memory a stonemason called Amun-pa-nefer admitted tunnelling into a royal tomb and stripping the pharaoh and his queen of gold, silver and precious stones:

We opened their coffins, and their coverings in which they were. We found the august mummy of this king. There was a numerous list of amulets and ornaments of gold at its throat; its head had a mask of gold upon it; the august mummy of this king was overlaid with gold throughout. Its coverings were wrought with gold and silver, within and without; inlaid with every costly stone. We stripped off the gold, which we found on the august mummy of this god, and its amulets and ornaments which were at its throat, and the covering wherein it rested. We found the king's wife likewise; we stripped off all that we found on her likewise. We set fire to their coverings. We stole their furniture, which we found with them, being vases of gold, silver, and bronze. We divided, and made the gold which we found on these two gods, on their mummies, and the amulets, ornaments and coverings, into eight parts.

Amun-pa-nefer then described the chain of corruption:

We then crossed over to Thebes. And after some days, the agents of Thebes heard that we had been stealing in the west, so they arrested me and imprisoned me at the mayor of Thebes' place. So I took the four pounds of gold that had fallen to me as my share, and gave them to Kha-em-Opet, the District Clerk of the harbour of Thebes. He let me go, and I joined my companions, and they made up for me another share. And I, as well as the other robbers who are with me, have continued to this day in the practice of robbing the tombs of the nobles and people of the land who rest in the west of Thebes. And a large number of the men of the land rob them also.

This wooden statue of a lion-headed deity was found in the plundered burial chamber of Amenophis II. The robbers left it behind after gouging out its eyes, which were probably of precious stones.

Presumably the bribe was shared out among other officials higher up the ladder, though no share fell to the mayor of Thebes who either was an honest man or complained because he was being cut out of the action.

In spite of this trial and others of which we have been left records, the situation went from bad to worse. The tomb of **Amenophis III** was broken into, and soon the priests were shifting the bodies of **Amosis I**, **Amenophis I**, **Tuthmosis II** and others from one tomb to another in a desperate effort to protect them. No fewer than thirteen royal mummies were taken to the tomb of **Amenophis II**, where they were found in modern times. Another thirty were collected from their various hiding places and were stacked in a shaft in a rocky cleft just outside the Valley of the Kings, where likewise they remained undisturbed for the next three thousand years.

The **tomb of Tutankhamun** had also been broken into, twice and possibly three times within a very few years of his death, but the robbers had been quickly spotted and caught or forced to run away, and their pilfering had been slight compared to the ruthless plundering during the troubled times of the 20th and 21st Dynasties. And then Tutankhamun's tomb vanished altogether beneath the debris and the huts of the workmen digging out the tomb of Ramses IV.

MODERN TOMB ROBBING

The modern heyday for tomb robbers was during the late nine teenth century with the explosion in Europe and America of archaeological and tourist interest in ancient Egypt. Luxor saw a roaring trade in tablets, statuettes and scarabs, both real and faked – home-made scarabs were fed to turkeys to 'acquire by the simple process of digestion a degree of venerableness that is really charming', wrote one visitor. Mummies were dragged out of their tombs and unrolled, stripped of their valuables, broken up and left to crumble in the sands. In earlier centuries, mummy cases were chopped up for firewood, and from at least the thirteenth century to the nineteenth century 'mummy' was highly regarded in Europe for its medicinal properties, the export demand sometimes proving so great that Egyptians often substituted modern corpses.

In 1875, Abdel Rasul, sheikh of the village of Gurna, found the cache of thirty mummies that had been hidden in the rocky cleft of the Theban hills by the desperate priests of the 21st Dynasty. The sheikh kept his find a secret for six years, selling off bits and pieces as he needed money. Archaeologists traced these clues to their source, and the mummies are those now on display in the Mummy Room of the Egyptian Museum in Cairo. As these long-dead pharaohs sailed down the Nile by steamer, Egyptians lined the banks at village after village, the women ululating in lament, the men firing their rifles in homage.

Today the authorities say that all 900 known tombs in the Valley of the Kings and the Theban necropolis have been checked and locked. But there are constant rumours of secret finds beneath the houses and even the wall paintings in known tombs are occasionally removed. Howard Carter was convinced that there was only one way to deal with the matter. Brushing aside critics who call archaeologists vandals for taking objects from the tombs, he argued that by being left in place they would sooner or later be stolen by thieves, and that would be the last seen of them, but that by removing them to museums, their safety was assured.

5. Resources and Glossary

Selkis, who along with her fellow goddesses Isis, Nephthys and Neith, stood as guardian at the golden shrine enclosing the sarcophagus of Tutankhamun

Further reading

The range of works on ancient Egypt is vast, particularly on the Old and New Kingdoms, and particularly on Tutankhamun and his likely father Akhenaten. This list is highly selective and includes mainly titles in print – though a few may require searching out at libraries.

GENERAL ANCIENT HISTORY

John Baines and Jaromir Malek Atlas of Ancient Egypt *Phaidon, o/p; Checkmark.* An atlas, yes, with superb maps and site plans, but also a wide-ranging encyclopedia on religion, art, pyramid building, burial customs, Nubia, women in society and so on, by two leading authorities in Egyptology.

James Henry Breasted A History of Egypt from the Earliest Times to the Persian Conquest *Simon Publications; 2 vols.* This first attempt at an all-encompassing narrative history of ancient Egypt down to 525 BC was first published in New York in 1905 and has gone through subsequent editions there and in London. Breasted, a great American Egyptologist, presents a vigorous and highly readable historical review which largely compensates for the out-of-dateness of his detail.

Rosalie and Antony E. David A Biographical Dictionary of Ancient Egypt *Routledge; Univ of Oklahoma.* A useful Who's Who of Egyptians down to the Arab conquest in the 7th century AD, and also covering important foreigners with whom they came into contact as well as classical writers who left vivid descriptions of the country.

Henri Frankfort Ancient Egyptian Religion: An interpretation *Dover.* Frankfort shows how the bewildering diversity and contradictions of Egyptian religion resolve into certain common and comprehensible themes, as meaningful today as in the ancient past.

George Hart A Dictionary of Egyptian Gods and Goddesses *Routledge.* As close to exhaustive as a pocket-sized volume can ever be, this comprehensive god-spotters' guide shows what they looked like, provides potted biographies and takes you through their various pseudonyms, guises and powers.

Sir Alan Gardiner Egypt of the Pharaohs, An Introduction *Oxford*

University Press. Though dedicated to Breasted, Gardiner's book (published in 1961) is more than an updating of narrative history – rather it emphasizes how knowledge of the past is achieved through the study and interpretation of ancient texts, many of which are quoted, allowing Egyptians of the past to speak for themselves.

Herodotus The Histories *Penguin.* Herodotus travelled to Egypt in about 447 BC, and the material he gathered there fills a good third of his great history of the Greeks and their world. He spoke with priests, asked how the pyramids had been built, enquired into the process of embalming the dead, observed the habits of peasant men and women, and sought the origins of the Nile, to present a vivid ethnographical and historical account of a country, unreliable but wonderful for its insatiable curiosity.

Barry J. Kemp Ancient Egypt, Anatomy of a Civilization (*Routledge*). Modern Egyptologists, rather than simply writing history, tend to prefer to interpret it with tendentious or moralizing results, but in this case the effect is stimulating.

Michael Rice Egypt's Legacy, The Archetypes of Western Civilization *Routledge.* Another go at interpreting what the ancient Egyptians were up to, this time with the benefit of some Jungian insights which can be stimulating – indeed, entertaining – but leave you unsure if Rice is entirely sound on matters strictly Egyptological.

Ian Shaw (ed.) **The Oxford History of Ancient Egypt** *Oxford University Press.* Published in 2000, this is the latest attempt to encompass the whole of ancient Egyptian history up to the end of the Roman period in a single volume. Chapters are arranged chronologically, though each chapter is more an essay than a strict narrative and does not always cover as much ground as one would like before fluttering off into some discursive realm. The predynastic and dynastic periods are handled very well, the Graeco-Roman period less so.

A.J. Spencer Death in Ancient Egypt *Penguin, o/p.* As well as examining the varieties of mummies, tombs and funeral rites, the reasons for their existence, and how they changed in response to religious developments, this book also shows how modern Egyptological techniques are able to trace family relationships among the dead, identify prevalent diseases and sometimes provide complete pathological case histories of individuals.

TUTANKHAMUN/NEW KINGDOM

Cyril Aldred Akhenaten, Pharaoh of Egypt *Thames & Hudson, o/p.* This is a comprehensive, authoritative and enthralling account of Akhenaten and his wife Nefertiti, of their revolutionary sun disc religion and the extraordinary art it produced, and of the calamitous aftermath.

Zahi Hawass Tutankhamun and the Golden Age of the Pharaohs *National Geographic*. This is the official companion book to the exhibition that has been sponsored by National Geographic magazine. Hawass, who is secretary general of Egypt's Supreme Council of Antiquities, is well placed to guide readers through the exhibition, and the llustrations are superb.

Erik Hornung Akhenaten and the Religion of Light *Cornell University Press*. Horning is Germany's leading expert on the Valley of the Kings and the 18th Dynasty, and much of that knowledge is distilled into this book about Akhenaten and his beliefs.

K.A. Kitchen Pharaoh Triumphant, The Life and Times of Ramesses II *Aris & Phillips*. Written by the eminent expert on Rameses the Great, this has all the readability and narrative drive of a good historical biography, and is no less vivid for treating a subject who lived over three thousand years ago.

Dominic Montserrat Akhenaten: History, Fantasy and Ancient Egypt *Routledge*. Montserrat does not so much offer up an account of Akhenaten and his period, as look at how others interpret the material too often for their own ends. He gives a useful account of what most authorities agree about on the late 18th-dynasty period, and then he examines the rest, which is where the fantasy comes in. This book is a wonderful corrective against going off

the historical deep end, something which Egyptology all too readily encourages. The book also covers the cultural reactions to the activities, finds and pronouncements of Egyptologists, and delves into some pretty murkish waters.

David O'Connor and Eric H. Cline Amenhotep III: Perspectives on his reign *University of Michigan*. A multifaceted examination of the times of Amenophis III during the apogee of the New Kingdom and the Egyptian Empire.

Nicholas Reeves Akhenaten: Egypt's False Prophet *Thames and Hudson*. Reeves takes issue with the view of Akhenaten that has held sway for over a century, that he was a persecuted idealist who founded a new faith. Instead, says Reeves, he used religion in a calculated attempt to gather power entirely into his hands. If you thought Akhenaten was St Francis of Assisi, you now find out that he was Saddam Hussein. This is an immensely readable and scholarly work from one of the world's leading experts in the period.

Nicholas Reeves The Complete Tutankhamun *Thames and Hudson*. While dealing fairly briefly with the search for the tomb, and with the broader historical period within which Tutankhamun's reign was set, as a study of Tutankhamun himself, and especially of his tomb and its contents, this book is unbeatable.

EGYPTOLOGY

Howard Carter The Tomb of Tut-Ankh-Amen. Carter was a wonderful writer, and his account is fully equal to the wonder of his discovery. It was first published in three volumes in 1923; numerous reprints have appeared in various forms over the years, most usually the first volume only, or sometimes an abridgement of all three volumes.

Geoffrey T. Martin The Hidden Tombs of Memphis *Thames and Hudson*. Saqqara has been described as the greatest archeological site in the world, so far only partly touched by the excavator's trowel and with many more secrets to reveal. In proof comes this publication, detailing discoveries of sites dating from the time of Tutankhamun and Rameses II.

H.V.F. Winstone Howard Carter and the Discovery of the Tomb of Tutankhamun *Constable, o/p*. Written with elegance and sensitivity, Winstone's book captures the difficult but remarkable character of Carter and thrillingly retells the story of his discovery of Tutankhamun's tomb.

Websites

Launch Tutankhamun into your search engine and you will come up with over a million hits – Tutmania, which began in the 1920s, is clearly alive and well. Here is a selection of some of the most interesting, informative, and odd.

Tutankhamun and the Golden Age of the Pharaohs
The official website for the current exhibition, with a gallery of photographs illustrating a number of the items on display and some background material
http://www.kingtut.org

Griffith Institute
This is where anyone seriously interested in Tutankhamun begins their researches, and carries them on -- the site is almost inexhaustible. Located in the Ashmolean Museum at Oxford, the Griffiths holds the complete records of Howard Carter's discovery of the tomb and is busily placing vast quantities of material online, including Carter's diaries, Harry Burton's magnificent photographs, and so on.
http://www.griffith.ashmus.ox.ac.uk/

Egypt Exploration Society
Originally named the Egypt Exploration Fund, this was the organisation that first sent Howard Carter to Egypt, employing him at Beni Hasan and then at Hatshepsut's mortuary temple at Deir el Bahri. Well over a hundred years old, its archives are impressive and its activities continue to be outstanding – for example it is conducting new excavations at Amarna, which the website wonderfully illustrates.
http://www.ees.ac.uk/

Egyptian Museum, Cairo
The Egyptian Museum's collection of its nation's antiquities is supreme in all the world. Its website conducts you through the galleries, from period to period, offering you thousands of images.
http://www.egyptianmuseum.gov.eg/

British Museum
The British Museum in London has one of the two or three greatest ancient Egypt collections in the world, and it has turned its website into a highly useful resource.
http://www.thebritishmuseum.ac.uk/

Metropolitan Museum of Art
The Metropolitan Museum in New York has the fienst Ancient Egyptian collection in the United States. And after Howard Carter discovered Tutankhamun's tomb, the Met provided

him with much needed additional expert assistance.
http://www.metmuseum.org/

Digital Egypt

The last word in Egyptological resources. Digitial Egypt has been designed for university students on ancient Egyptian courses, and amounts to thousands upon thousands of pages. Organised by University College, London, it is a feast.
http://www.digitalegypt.ucl.ac.uk/

BBC Ancient Egypt website

This is a remarkably good site on ancient Egypt in all its aspects, with in depths articles by renowned authorities, all wonderfully illustrated. There are specific sections on Tutankhamun and the Amarna period.
http://www.bbc.co.uk/history/ancient/egyptians/

Al Ahram Weekly

This is the English-language online weekly version of Egypt's respected daily newspaper *Al Ahram*. It has a good search engine and a large archive of excellent feature articles, many of course to do with Egyptology.
http://weekly.ahram.org.eg/

Old World New World

An American website which covers the archaeological aspects of Tutankhamun, particularly the involvement of such US institutions as the Metropolitan Museum of Art in New York, but also the effect of Tutankhamun on cinema, literature and popular culture generally.
http://xroads.virginia.edu/~UG00/rekas/tut/main.htm

Gavin's Egyptomania

A rather wonderful and eclectic British website devoted to the archaeology of ancient Egypt but also to its popular spinoffs in art, architecture, music, design and advertising, not to mention coverage of vintage Egypt in the late nineteenth and early twentieth centuries through postcards, stereocards, the *Illustrated London News*, and other ephemera. Well worth a browse.
http://web.ukonline.co.uk/gavin.egypt/

Steve Martin's Tut Song

If Tutankhamun were not dead yet, this would kill him. To find it, key "King Tut Steve Martin" into YouTube's search engine.
http://www.youtube.com

Glossary

Amun God of Thebes; as Amun-Ra he was associated with the sun god and became the national god during the New Kingdom. His sacred animal was the ram. Along with his wife, Mut, and their son, Khonsu, Amun was one of the Theban triad.

Ankh The hieroglyphic sign for life, resembling a cross with a loop in place of the upper arm.

Anubis God of the dead, associated with interment. His sacred animal was the dog or jackal.

Aten The sun's disc; the life force. Worshipped by Akhenaten as the one god.

Atum A sun god of Heliopolis, creator of the universe, often combined with Ra and represented as a man.

Ba A spirit that inhabits the body during life but is not attached to it; at death it leaves the body and joins the divine spirit (*see* ka).

Benben The primeval hill which first arose from the waters.

Book of the Dead The generic name given to a variable collection of spells (including for example the Amduat and the Book of the Gates) which from New Kingdom to Ptolemaic times were written on papyrus and buried with the mummy. They continue the tradition of the Pyramid Texts such as at the Pyramid of Unas and the funerary texts on tomb walls in the Valley of the Kings.

Canopic jars Containers placed within ancient tombs to preserve those organs and viscera thought essential for the dead man's continued existence in the afterlife.

Cartouche In hieroglyphics, the oval band enclosing the god's or pharaoh's name and symbolising unchanging continuity.

Colossus A greater than life-size statue, usually of a king.

Colours Primary colours usually had particular applications and significance in ancient Egyptian painting. Black represented death: mummies, also Osiris as king of the dead, were commonly depicted in black. Blue was for sky and water, the sky gods painted this colour. Green was the colour of rebirth: Osiris, who overcame death and was reborn, often had his face and limbs painted green; also the solar disc was commonly painted light green on sarcophagi, instead of its usual red.

Red was for blood and fire; men's bodies were depicted as reddish brown or brown; it also had a maleficent connotation: Seth was painted reddish brown. White represented silver and was the colour of the moon; it was also the colour of the garments of the gods and the crown of Upper Egypt. Yellow represented gold and was also used as the colour for women's bodies until the mid–18th Dynasty; thereafter the only women painted this colour were goddesses.

Crowns The red flat-topped crown of Lower Egypt was joined with the tall white crown of Upper Egypt to represent unification of the country (*see* colours). The blue crown or headdress was worn when riding a chariot; it appears after the introduction of the horse into Egypt by the Hyksos c.1600 BC. No matter what headdress the pharaoh wore, he was always shown with the uraeus on his forehead.

Faience Glazed earthenware, often decorated, formed as pottery or in blocks or tiles as a wall facing.

Fellahin Egyptian peasants. The singular is fellah.

Geb Personification of the earth.

Heb-Sed The jubilee marking the thirtieth year of a pharaoh's reign.

Herakhte A form of Horus, 'Horus of the horizon', often combined with the sun god as Ra-Herakhte and so wor-

shipped at Heliopolis. The falcon was sacred to him.

Horus The son of Isis and Osiris, and revered as the sun god. He was represented as the sun disc or a falcon, his sacred animal.

Hyksos A foreign people who ruled Egypt from Avaris in the Delta during the Second Intermediate Period. Probably Semites and possibly a displaced ruling caste from Palestine, they did not introduce a new culture but rather respected and encouraged Egyptian civilisation and its institutions. Nevertheless, the propaganda of the Theban princes who ejected the Hyksos from the country, initiating the New Kingdom, made the period of Hyksos rule synonymous with anarchy and destruction.

Hypostyle A hypostyle hall is any chamber whose ceiling is supported by columns or pillars.

Isis Sister and wife to Osiris, mother of Horus. She is often shown with a throne on her head.

Ithyphallic Denoting the erect phallus of a depicted god or pharaoh, most commonly the god Min, but also Amun. It was a sign of fertility.

Ka A spirit that inhabits the body during life and may leave it in death, but requires the continued existence of the body (hence mummification, or by substitution, ka statues) for its survival. The ka was personal and individual, in a sense the ideal image of a man's own life (see ba).

Khonsu Son of Amun and Mut; god of the moon. The falcon was sacred to him.

Maat The goddess of truth, whose symbol was the ostrich feather. Maat is actually the deification of a concept which Egyptians strove for, both personally and for the state. As well as truth, one can attempt to define it as justice, correctness, balance. The best definition is the now rare English word meet.

Min The god of the harvest, frequently amalgamated with Amun. He was ithyphallically represented, that is shown with an erection. The Greeks identified him with Pan.

Mont A Theban god of war, represented with a falcon's head.

Mut The wife of Amun and mother of Khonsu. Her sacred animal was the vulture.

Necropolis Greek for cemetery, literally city (polis) of the dead (necros).

Neith Goddess of Sais, shown wearing the red crown of Lower Egypt. She was one of the goddesses who protected the dead and the Canopic jars.

Nephthys Sister of Isis and Osiris, married to Seth; with outstretched wings one of the protector goddesses of the dead, guardian of the Canopic jars.

Nome An administrative province of ancient Egypt. The chief official of a nome was the nomarch.

Nut Goddess of the sky, often shown supported by Shu.

Opening of the Mouth Funerary ceremony by which the mouth of the mummy was symbolically opened to ensure it could partake of nourishment in the afterlife.

Osiris Originally a vegetation god, later the lord of the underworld. Murdered and dismembered by Seth, he was the husband and brother of Isis and father of Horus.

Papyrus A plant identified with Lower Egypt; it served as a writing material from I Dyn to Islamic times.

Ptah The patron god of Memphis and father of the gods. His sacred animal was the Apis bull.

Pylon Arranged in pairs, forming a monumental gateway to a temple. Where there are several sets of pylons, each preceding a court, they descend in size as the sanctuary of the god is approached, while the floor level rises, creating a focussing or tunnelling effect.

Ra The sun god, usually combined with another god, such as Atum-Ra, Amun-Ra or Ra-Herakhte. His priesthood was at Heliopolis.

Selkis Scorpion goddess, often shown with a scorpion on her head; she was a guardian of the dead.

Seth God of chaos, brother and slayer of Osiris, adversary of Horus, he became a god of war. His sacred animal was possibly the aardvark.

Shabti A mummiform figurine, serving in the tomb as deputy for the dead man, carrying out his labour obligations.

Shu The god of the air. He is often shown supporting Nut.

Stele An upright stone slab or pillar with an inscription or design, used as a monument or grave marker.

Theban triad Amun, his wife Mut and their son Khonsu.

Thoth A moon deity and the god of science. The ibis and baboon were sacred to him.

Uraeus The cobra worn on the forehead of a pharoah as both an emblem and an instrument of protection, breathing flames and destroying enemies.

Index

Index

Cover images

Front cover image Tutankhamun © Corbis
Back cover images © Michael Haag

Photo Credits

AKG-Images/Ullstein Bild: 14, 21, 51; Ancient Art and Architecture: 23; Archivio Iconografico S.A./Corbis: 24; Associated Press: 175; Bettmann/Corbis: 72; Bridgeman Art Library: 190; Egyptian National Museum, Cairo/Bridgeman Art Library: 28, 33, 37, 40, 190; Werner Forman/Corbis: 32, 107; Griffith Institute, Oxford: 10, 26, 27, 29 left, 29 right, 30, 31, 35, 36 above, 36 below, 39, 41, 42, 44, 55, 58, 61, 62, 63, 65, 67, 71, 74, 77, 84, 85 above, 85 below, 87, 89, 92 above, 92 below, 93 above, 93 below, 164, 169, 171, 173, 178, 180, 191; Michael Haag: 9, 25, 95, 98, 105, 109, 114, 117, 122, 127, 128, 130, 131, 133, 137, 138, 141, 142, 155, 156, 158, 166, 184, 195, 198; Herzog Foundation: 13; Highclere Castle (Carnarvon Archive): 47; Stapleton Collection/Corbis: 80; Ruggero Vanni/Corbis: 135; Sandro Vannini/Corbis: 14, 34; Gavin Watson: ; Roger Wood/Corbis: 145.

Publications

G. Daressy, *Fouilles de la vallée des rois (Catalogue général des antiquités égyptiennes du musée du Caire)* 1902: 203; Theodore M. Davis, *Tomb of Queen Tiyi,* 1910: 22, 160, 201; Elliot Smith, *The Royal Mummies (Catalogue général antiquités égyptiennes du musée du Caire),* 1912: 119; *rated London News:* 38, 68, 83, 196; J.E. Quibell, *Tomb aa and Thuiu (Catalogue général des antiquités égypti- u musée du Caire),* 1908: 199 left, 199 right.

Index